To

_____

From

_____

Looking Up Devotional

© 2014 by Beth Moore

Published in Nashville, Tennessee, by Thomas Nelson®.

Cover design by Bruce DeRoos.

Unless otherwise indicated, all Scripture quotations are taken from THE HOLY BIBLE, NEW INTERNATIONAL VERSION®. Copyright © 1973, 1978, 1984, 2011 by Biblica, Inc.™ Used by permission. All rights reserved worldwide. www.zondervan.com

Scripture quotations marked NLT are taken from the *Holy Bible*, New Living Translation, copyright © 1996, 2004, 2007 by Tyndale House Foundation. Used by permission of Tyndale House Publishers, Inc., Carol Stream, Illinois 60188. All rights reserved.

Scripture quotations marked HCSB are taken from the Holman Christian Standard Bible®. © 1999, 2000, 2002, 2003 by Broadman and Holman Publishers. All rights reserved.

Scripture quotations marked ESV are taken from THE ENGLISH STANDARD VERSION. © 2001 by Crossway Bibles, a division of Good News Publishers. Used by Permission.

Scripture quotations marked ASV are taken from the American Standard Version, BibleGateway.com.

Scripture quotations marked AMP are taken from the Amplified® Bible. Copyright © 1954, 1958, 1962, 1964, 1965, 1987 by The Lockman Foundation. Used by permission. (www.Lockman.org)

Scripture quotations marked NKJV are taken from the New King James Version®. Copyright © 1982 by Thomas Nelson, Inc. Used by permission. All rights reserved.

Scripture quotations marked NASB are taken from the NEW AMERICAN STANDARD BIBLE®, Copyright © 1960,1962,1963,1968,1971,1972,1973,1975,1977, 1995 by The Lockman Foundation. Used by permission. (www.Lockman.org)

Thomas Nelson titles may be purchased in bulk for educational, business, fund-raising, or sales promotional use. For information, please e-mail SpecialMarkets@ ThomasNelson.com.

ISBN-13: 978-0-7180-2165-8

Printed in China

15 16 17 18 DSC 6 5 4 3

www.thomasnelson.com

Looking Up

Devotional

Trusting
God With
Your Every
Need

BETH MOORE

WITH LISA GUEST

Devotional content formerly published as part
of *Looking Up Devotional Journal*, based on
Get Out of That Pit © 2009 by Beth Moore.

THOMAS NELSON
Since 1798

NASHVILLE   MEXICO CITY   RIO DE JANEIRO

Every person can know the complete
redemption of Jesus Christ, purpose
for life, and fullness of joy.

I waited patiently for the Lord;
he turned to me and heard my cry.

He lifted me out of the slimy pit,
out of the mud and mire;
he set my feet on a rock
and gave me a firm place to stand.

He put a new song in my mouth,
a hymn of praise to our God.
many will see and fear the Lord
and put their trust in him.

Psalm 40:1–3

Introduction

*M*y life passion is to encourage people to come to know and love Jesus Christ through the study of His Word. My life message within that passion, however, is complete and glorious freedom. The kind only Christ can bring. I do not know why but it has never been enough for me to be free. I want you to be free too. It is not enough for me to know the thrill of God's presence. I want you to know it too. I want you to know the power of His Word that can defy every addiction, heal any affliction, and plug up every pit. I want you to know a love that is better than life.

I believe God has scheduled a time and a way for you to get out of your pit. You're going to need to show up for it though. My prayer is that what follows will serve as an itinerary and guide. If you'll grant me the privilege, I'd like to be your attendant for a while. I've taken this trip before. It's bumpy but the destination is worth it. Thanks for having me along.

You really can move up and out of that pit.

Beth

The Lord will vindicate me;
your love, Lord, endures forever—
do not abandon the works of your hands.

Psalm 138:8

*L*ife can be excruciating. Crushing, in fact. The sheer magnitude of our worries can press down on our heads until we unknowingly descend into a pit of despair one inch at a time. Something so horrible can happen that we conclude we'll never be okay again. We can blow it so badly we think God would just as soon we stayed under that dirt and out of His sight.

But the Bible teaches that there are no lost causes. No permanent pit-dwellers except those who refuse to leave. Every person can know the complete redemption of Jesus Christ, a purpose for life, and a fullness of joy. No, life won't ever be easy, but the trade-off is a spin around Planet Earth that actually means something.

I am convinced that when the last chapter of each life story is recorded in the annals of heaven, people would rather have lived out their fullness of days with purpose rather than painlessness.

Living with purpose requires energy and focus, time and sacrifice. What keeps you from pursuing a more purpose-filled life? Are you willing to release those things to the Lord and allow Him to empower you to fulfill the purpose He has for you?

Lord God, how wonderful that we can live our days on this planet with purpose—and how wonderful that when You call us to fulfill that purpose, You empower us as well! I ask for that power, Lord. Whether I'm living out my purpose by being a wife, a mother, a friend, an ambassador for You, a servant, or a worker in the marketplace, may I find in You strength and joy.

Since you are my rock and my fortress,
for the sake of your
name lead and guide me.

Psalm 31:3

If you're in a pit, you don't have to stay in it. Even if you've been there your whole life, you can call it a day. Even if you somehow—at least in your own mind—deserve the pit you live in, you're still not stuck there.

Maybe you're the noble type trying to make the best of your pit. You keep wondering why you can't get satisfied there, why you aren't mature enough to be content where you are. After all, didn't the apostle Paul tell us that we should learn to be content in any circumstance?

Has it occurred to you that maybe a pit is one place where you're not supposed to be content? Maybe you should thank God you're not. Some things weren't meant to be accepted. A pit is one of them. Quit trying to make the best of it. It's time to get out.

Will you think outside the box—outside the pit—and accept the truth that God doesn't want you in there any longer?

I praise You, Lord, for being my Deliverer, my Rescuer, my Redeemer! I know I'm not supposed to be content in my pit. And I believe You can get me out—You want me out—of it. I will look to You to give me strength and to lead me to a place of true contentment.

$\mathcal{M}$y husband, our two dogs, and I travel a lot, and we're often asked why we don't get an RV. The answer: the bathroom. The small space and lack of fresh air in an RV makes the presence of a bathroom so . . . well . . . inescapable. They say you get used to it, but do I really want to? Nope, the way I see it, we were not meant to get used to some things. Like living in a pit.

Let's say for years you've been living in an old RV so small you can't stretch your legs or stand up straight. Then imagine being offered a brand-new home. A real one on a solid foundation with big closets and wide-open spaces. You can hardly wait to move in. Filled with anticipation, you rev up the motor of the old RV and plow it right into the new living room, taking out a wall or two on the way. Ah, finally! A new place to call home! You settle back in your RV seat, take a deep breath, and then it hits you. That deep breath tasted a lot like that old lavatory.

Friend, what is the cry of your heart today? God really does have the tools to unhitch that mobile pit from you. He also has a firm place for you where you can stand. And, yes, He hears your cry!

You are gentle and powerful, patient and loving . . . and nothing is impossible for You, Lord God! So I ask You—who hears me whenever I call out for you and for whom nothing is impossible—to unhitch that mobile pit of mine!

> *"For I know the plans I have for you,"* declares
> the LORD, *"plans to prosper you and not to harm
> you, plans to give you hope and a future."*
>
> Jeremiah 29:11

In our Christian subculture, we think a pit of sin is the only kind of pit there is. But we have to think much more broadly. For starters, I see in God's Word three ways we can get into a pit.

First, you know you are in a pit when you feel stuck, and you can't get yourself out. David's pit was "slimy," muddy, and miry (Psalm 40:2), and Jeremiah "sank down" in his (Jeremiah 38:6).

Second, you know you are in a pit when you can't stand up . . . against your enemy. In other words, a pit is an early (figurative) grave that Satan digs for you in hopes he can bury you alive. Satan can't make you stay there, but God will not make you leave.

And you know you are in a pit when you've lost vision . . . because pits have no windows. In that darkness, we can no longer see things that may have once been obvious to us. Also, the close confinement of a pit exhausts us with the endless echo of self-absorption. We can't see out, so we turn our sights in, and that nearsightedness breeds hopelessness.

Isn't it crazy that even the painful but familiar can be comfortable? It may be comfortable, but it's *never* God's best for you!

Thank You that You are a loving God who wants what's best for me—and a wise God who knows what's best for me! And this pit isn't it, Lord. So please help me get out. Start showing me how to get out—help me want to get out!

I pray that your hearts will be flooded with light
so that you can understand the confident hope
he has given to those he called—his holy people
who are his rich and glorious inheritance.

Ephesians 1:18 NLT

Created in the image of God, we are intended to overflow with effervescent life, stirring and spilling with God-given vision. That's partly what the apostle Paul was talking about when he prayed that the eyes of our hearts would be enlightened in order that we might know the hope to which Christ has called us (Ephesians 1:18). The Amplified Bible calls it "having the eyes of your heart flooded with light." That's what you miss in the pit.

Our imaginations were fashioned like wicks to be ignited by the fire of fresh revelation, dripping with wax that God can imprint with His endless signatures. In the light of God's face shining upon us, we also glimpse reflections of our true selves. We were meant to see ourselves as part of something vital, something incredibly thrilling. But the eyes of some of us have adjusted to the darkness of the pit surrounding us. The resulting dim vision ages us rapidly, and we lose the childlikeness that once made us feel like real princes and princesses in a kingdom. We can be young and yet feel old. Heavy laden. Burdened. In a pit where vision is lost and dreams are foolishness.

What dreams do you need to once again pursue? Know that God's Light can enable you to do exactly that.

Lord God, help me regain a sense of hope for the future . . . wonder at the gift of life . . . and joy in Your amazing grace and love for me.

*Y*ou can get thrown into a pit. That's right, without doing one thing to deserve it and without wallowing your way into it. I'm not talking about a pit of sin here. This one's a pit of innocence—the kind a lot of believers don't realize exists. You can get thrown right into the miry deep before you know what hit you. Or, worse yet, before you know *who* hit you. In fact, those were the very circumstances surrounding the first pit ever mentioned in Scripture. Genesis 37:23–25 records the details:

When Joseph came to his brothers, they stripped off his robe, the robe of many colors that he had on. Then they took him and threw him into the pit. The pit was empty; there was no water in it. Then they sat down to eat a meal. (HCSB)

Of all the ways to get into a pit, getting thrown in—by some*thing* but especially by some*one*—can be the most complicated to deal with emotionally and spiritually. Drunk drivers, a violent criminal, a loved one suffering from mental illness or alcoholism, divorce, disease, a special needs child, a house fire, a stock market crash, the death of a child—the list of ways we can get thrown into a pit goes on and on.

Facing the truth about your pit will set you free—the truth about how difficult and painful certain chapters of your life have been and truth about how God can and does absolutely redeem those times.

Lord, may the darkness of the pit I was thrown into make Your faithful deliverance appear that much brighter and more radiant with love and hope.

> *Lead me, LORD, in your righteousness*
> *because of my enemies—*
> *make your way straight before me.*
>
> Psalm 5:8

*A*gain, of all the ways to get into a pit, getting thrown in—by some*thing* but especially by some*one*—can be the most complicated to deal with emotionally and spiritually. For starters, when someone throws us in, we've obviously got someone to blame: *It's all that person's fault.* Talk about a scenario with the capacity to eat us alive!

You want to talk complications? Okay, how about times when you've been thrown into the pit by someone else's sin—and that someone happens to be a family member? Or a loved one who was supposed to love you back? Getting over the trauma would have been hard enough had Joseph been thrown into the pit by strangers who picked him randomly. Instead, his own flesh and blood did it—and they did it intentionally. Been there? Me too.

And what about the times when a person has been used by the enemy to throw us into a pit, and he or she remains close by, lives on as if nothing has happened, sees our distress and anguish, but will not hear us? Maybe even despise us for our weakness? Ah, that's complicated. I know from experience.

The God of all compassion knows your complicated situation as well as your aching heart, and He is at work in both for your good.

Father God, acknowledging how tough it is to be in this pit isn't hard. The assignment to stop blaming the one who threw me into this pit is very hard. Help me to do what I can't do on my own.

See to it that no one falls short of the grace of God and that no bitter root grows up to cause trouble and defile many.

Hebrews 12:15

Beloved, I hate to have to bring up this word, but I just don't have a choice. It's the last word any of us wants to hear echoing back and forth in a pit we've been thrown into. You already know what this word is, and you're probably sick of hearing it. But we have to hear that difficult word again: *forgive*. It's a tough thing to do, but we've got to forgive, even—no, *especially*—those who don't care to be forgiven.

You think you can't forgive? I felt the same way. I heard over and over how I'd have to forgive, but in a huff I just folded my arms over my chest and refused to do anything about it. You see, I started out in a pit of innocence, but through the years my bitterness rearranged the furniture until it was nothing more than a well-camouflaged pit of sin. But I thought forgiving my pit-throwers would make what happened all right. But, to be sure, it didn't. Still hasn't. What I didn't understand about forgiveness was that it would make me all right. One day I finally began getting that message, and I'm praying right now that this is that day for you.

Like all of God's commands, His call to forgive is for your good. Forgiveness is a process, and that process leads to freedom. Your freedom.

Lord, I want to obey Your command to forgive; I want to know the freedom that results. Help me on both counts!

[God] is able to do immeasurably more than all we ask or imagine, according to his power that is at work within us.

Ephesians 3:20

*R*eading one devotional on forgiveness does not enable us to extend total, permanent grace to the pit-throwers in our life. So I want to tell you a few things that have helped me in my ascent out of the pit of unforgiveness.

First, God changed the way I looked at the entire situation when I began to see that my grudge against people who hurt me only strengthened the grip of my bondage to them. Our grudges only work to further entangle and enmesh us with the persons we won't forgive. When we won't forgive, the people we often want to be around least because they've hurt us so badly are the very people we take with us emotionally everywhere we go!

I'll tell you something else that helped me greatly.

I began to look at forgiveness as tremendous empowerment, not as spineless passivity. My breakthrough came when I realized that nothing took more divine power than forgiving; therefore nothing is more powerful than forgiving. You will never use the force of your will more dramatically than when you agree with God to start forgiving. Forgiveness is not about feeling. It's about willing. No stronger force exists.

Forgiveness is power. First you will it and soon you'll feel it. Start today. Confirm it tomorrow. And keep confirming it by faith as the will of God for you in Christ Jesus.

Say this truth out loud: "Forgiveness is power." It truly is power over the grip that the past has on you and over the enemy who wants to keep you in your pit.

It is truly amazing, Almighty God, that the power of the Resurrection is available to me. May it enable me to choose to embrace the power of forgiveness.

Then I heard a loud voice in heaven say . . .
"The accuser of our brothers and sisters,
who accuses them before our God day
and night, has been hurled down."

Revelation 12:10

We tend to blame people we feel were used by Satan to throw us into a pit. But haven't most of us also felt the sickening urge toward self-blame? *It's all my fault.* That self-blame is often prompted by our own self-loathing. Satan the accuser knows that even when we're innocent of any reason for being in a pit, we are well aware that we are far from innocent in other things.

So maybe the question is not "Have you done anything wrong?" Maybe the better question is "Have you done the wrong that fits the pit?" If you have, well, so have I, and we'll deal with that. But if you've haven't, you're in a pit of innocence . . . whether or not you're innocent in every other area of your life.

Satan is a master at using our own insecurity against us. He knows that deep in our hearts we're so fragile and injured by life that, with his faintest whisper, we can feel guilty even when we're not. We've got some problems all right, but problems by themselves don't dig pits. They just offer shovels. We provide the sweat.

What problems are prompting you to provide the sweat and dig a pit for yourself? Fragile and injured by life, we are blessed to be able to run to the God of truth for healing, hope, and comfort.

Thank You, Almighty God, that You will defeat my accuser. In the meantime, help me stand strong in the truth that You love me so that I might recognize and rebuke my enemy's lies.

> *"With everlasting kindness
> I will have compassion on you,"
> says the LORD your Redeemer.*
>
> Isaiah 54:8

ow be honest with me. Have you visited the place of *It's all God's fault?* It's probably the most complicated place of all, but if we really want out of our pit, that visit is unavoidable. What do we do when we feel God is to blame for the pit we're in? Like when we've lost a loved one or lost our health? The problem with blaming God is that it charges Him with wrongdoing. Thankfully, He understands us and He takes into account our limitations: we are totally incapable of understanding His ways at times.

Can we really be sure that God always has our best interests at heart? If we're willing to stay close enough to Him and watch Him long enough, we will discover that the answer to the question is emphatically *yes.* The

Judge of all the earth will do right. He is complete perfection. All wise. Only good. But Satan has no more effective weapon in his arsenal than to make us question not so much whether God exists, but whether God is really good. For Satan to talk us into distrusting God and distancing ourselves from Him is to keep us broken and ineffective.

Bottom line, I can't explain how the whole goodness-of-God, suffering-of-man thing works, but I know that God cannot—does not—wrong His children. He can't. Inconceivably holy, God cannot sin. God is huge, God is wise, and God will redeem.

You know, Creator God, that I am but dust. You know, omniscient Lord, the doubts that cross my mind and even lodge in my heart. Yet in Your compassion, You accept me, You comfort me, and You promise to redeem life's hard times.

> *We know that all things work together for good to those who love God, to those who are the called according to His purpose.*
>
> Romans 8:28 NKJV

Think back on Joseph, our first scriptural example of a pit-dweller and one who did not dig his way into it. Somewhere along the way, Joseph decided not only to look up but also to point up. His decision to view God as entirely sovereign and ultimately responsible was the life of him. Why? Because he knew God could only be good and could do only right. The words Joseph spoke over his guilty brothers have been medicine to many sick souls: "You intended to harm me, but God intended it for good to accomplish what is now being done, the saving of many lives" (Genesis 50:20).

That word *intended* comes from the same Hebrew word translated "think" in Jeremiah 29:11: "For I know the thoughts that I think toward you, says the LORD, thoughts of peace and not of evil, to give you a future and a hope"(NKJV). God thinks of His children continually. And when God thinks of His children, He only thinks in terms of what can be used toward our good, toward His plan for us, and toward the future. God did not haphazardly or accidentally let Joseph's brothers throw him in the pit. He had thought it out in advance. He had looked at the good it could ultimately accomplish, the lives that could be helped and even saved. Then, and only then, in His sovereign purpose did He permit such harm to come to His beloved child. Had the incident not possessed glorious purpose, God would have disarmed it.

By God's grace, what good have you experienced— what glorious purpose have you glimpsed—from a bad situation or a season of suffering? Remember, God never changes. He who brought good out of that bad situation is in the very same business today, whatever your pit.

Lord, I believe; help my unbelief. And thank You for the spark of hope You have kindled in my heart.

Thanks be to God, who always leads us as captives in Christ's triumphal procession and uses us to spread the aroma of the knowledge of him everywhere.

2 Corinthians 2:14

Can you think of anything more evil than child abuse? When I was a little girl, God already knew the plans He had for me . . . just as He knew the plans He had for you. In His sovereignty, He allowed a series of wrongs to come to me that had mammoth effects on my life. For many years I reaped the whirlwind of negative consequences—and then I piled all manner of sin onto my victimization. Then one day, at the bottom of my pit, I raised my weary head and dirty, tear-streaked face to the sky. And redemption drew nigh. God knew the plans He had for me, and I have already lived long enough to see beauty exceed the ashes and divine pleasure exceed the pain.

Oh, beloved, you keep thinking about how life might have been had *that* not happened. But it's your wealth of experience that makes you rich. Spend it on hurting people. People in your workplace and your neighborhood are dying for hope. Dying to know there's a God . . . and that He's *for* them, not against them.

As God's people, we are blessed by Him so that we can be a blessing to others, and He uses life's hard times to make us even more valuable blessings to others.

Lord, how I long for the time when beauty will exceed the ashes and divine pleasure will exceed the pain. As I wait on Your timing for that season, please give me glimpses of the redemptive work You are doing in my heart and in my life.

> *"For my thoughts are not your thoughts, neither are your ways my ways," declares the LORD.*
>
> Isaiah 55:8

*L*ife is hard. Most of us have reasons to lie down in life and never get up. You've been through your stuff; I've been through mine. In one way or another, at one time or another, by one person or another, each of us has been thrown into a pit. Most of us can rationalize staying angry, bitter, or fearful and insecure for the rest of our lives. Most of us can talk others into not blaming us for being in our pit. We think we want people to lie down next to us, feel what we feel, and give us permission to stay there. But if they do, they help talk us into making ourselves at home in the early grave Satan dug for us. They agree to our living death.

Christ got down next to us in the grave, stayed the

better part of three days, and then got up . . . so we'd have permission to get up too. And start living life.

Beloved, let this one sink in deeply: if God allowed you to be thrown into a pit, you weren't picked on; you were picked out. God entrusted that suffering to you because He has faith in you. Live up to it. All the way up.

Let me guess. That statement stopped you dead in your tracks. Talk to God today about your thoughts, your feelings, and His decision to entrust certain suffering to you.

Lord God, You know without my telling You that I'm less than excited about the gift of suffering, but I am going to choose to believe that You will show me how to "live up to it" and that we will celebrate the good You bring out of it.

*Y*ou can slip in. That's the second way you can find yourself in a pit. Unlike the pit we get thrown into, we put ourselves into this one. But here's the catch: we didn't mean to. We just weren't watching where we were going. We got a little distracted. The path didn't seem bad; it just seemed new. We thought we were still okay, but the next thing we knew we were in a hole, our feet ankle deep in mud.

Yes, you got into this pit yourself, but it certainly wasn't planned. It wasn't what you wanted. You didn't mean for things to turn out the way they did. You didn't see it coming, but now you're in a hole.

You'd give anything if someone else had thrown you in, because you hate being the one to blame. In fact, at first you tried to think it was somebody—anybody—else's fault. But that sick feeling in your stomach tells you that, no matter who else was involved, nobody pushed you into this pit. You got yourself into this one. And you're not even sure how.

David hated getting himself into a pit. Read Psalm 38:4–6, 9–10, 12, and 14–17. Which of the feelings he described have you experienced in your pit?

Compassionate God, I hate feeling like a fool, and that's how I feel when I slip into a pit. Please bind the enemy; keep him from feeding that fire with his lies. And help me get out of this pit!

May the God of hope fill you with all
joy and peace as you trust in him,
so that you may overflow with hope
by the power of the Holy Spirit.

Romans 15:13

*H*aven't we all ended up in places we never meant to go? Can't we find fellowship in the suffering of slipping into a gosh-awful mess? Ironically, nothing makes us feel more alone than being in a pit, yet we've got enough underground company there to displace the overpopulation of West Texas gophers and leave them homeless for years. You just can't see all those underground neighbors because of your own pit wall.

You see, I've lived long enough to know that no one has it easy. Every person deals with secret pain. Private hurts. Some of those aches have gone on for a long time. On a bad day, as Proverbs 13:12 says, our hope can seem deferred and our heart, sick.

At first glance, we might be tempted to think such a pit of despair is not a pit of sin, but the apostle Paul would beg to differ. Despair is not just sadness. It's not healthy grief. It is hopelessness. We who have Christ possess the very essence of hope. Hopelessness means we've believed the evil one's report over God's. If we don't put our hope in God, we can talk ourselves into a pit. Remember, all a pit requires is that you feel stuck, that you feel you can't stand up effectively to your enemy, and that your vision of God's truth about you and about Him and about reality is slowly failing. Beware!

Hopelessness means we've believed the evil one's report about us, about God, about our circumstances. Become deaf to that report by instead putting your hope in God.

Holy Spirit, please fill my heart and my mind with hope, that I may know joy and peace—and stay far away from the slippery edge of a pit.

*Be alert and of sober mind. Your enemy
the devil prowls around like a roaring
lion looking for someone to devour.*

1 Peter 5:8

I'll soon get more specific about how to get out of a pit, but right now I want you to consider that one of the most priceless gifts we can bring out of our pit is newfound knowledge. Simply put, we can be a whole lot smarter coming out than we were going in. If we're willing, we can come out of the pit smartened up to Satan's agenda.

We can also tell on him to anyone who will listen. That's what I'm trying to do. When Scripture speaks of the devil's schemes, it speaks of a well-contrived program based on a step-by-step progressive plan (Ephesians 6:10–12). Though he tailors the specifics to fit individual weaknesses, I believe Satan's basic progressive plan remains consistent:

distraction ⇨ addiction ⇨ destruction.

Satan's definitive goal is to reap destruction, but that's rarely his starting point. His usual opening is distraction, and Scripture calls a small distraction that becomes a big distraction a *stronghold*. Anything that becomes a bigger preoccupation in your mind than the truth and knowledge of God is a stronghold. A stronghold can lead to an addiction, but Satan doesn't stop there. Addiction is not his goal. Destruction is.

To wise up to Satan's progressive plan, we want to discern the early warning signals of dangerous distraction and be onto him. After all, Satan capitalizes on an area of ignorance and detours a healthy drive into a deep ditch.

Thank You, Lord, for sharing with me Satan's strategy. That knowledge is empowering. Even more so is the presence of Your Holy Spirit within me. Thank You for not leaving me alone in my efforts to be alert to and stand strong against the enemy.

Do not quench the Spirit.

1 Thessalonians 5:19 NASB

Satan is a master at what he does, but he is not without limits. Listen carefully: if you belong to Christ, Satan cannot destroy you. The best he can do is to convince you that you're destroyed. No, beloved, you're not. No matter what's happened. No matter how foolish you've been. No matter how far you've gone. Wise up. The enemy is lying to you. Yes, he may have inflicted some tremendous losses. He may even have destroyed your job and torn apart some precious relationships—at least for now. But out of the unfathomable mercies of God, what you stand to gain if you're willing to lift up your empty hands to Him is astonishing.

But you and I have got to be onto the enemy's schemes from the start. We need desperately to discern when our souls take the first hit and make an immediate adjustment. Bow out of a situation or relationship you sense is dangerous and destructive. Set up safeguards and automatic accountability if you face temptation. Better yet, flee! Live in the light.

The last thing God wants is for you and me to live in fear. We don't want to be afraid, but we've got to be alert. If you're in Christ, you have a built-in alarm system. The Holy Spirit is in us, and if we don't quench Him, He'll tell us early on when we're headed for trouble. He'll also tell us whether to be careful right where we are or to bail out altogether.

Sometimes the Spirit's warning may not make any human sense. But mind what the Holy Spirit tells you even if you don't know why. You may live for years without clear understanding, but you can praise God, knowing He veered your path in a different direction to keep you out of some kind of ditch.

Thank You, Lord, for protecting me from the enemy. Make me sensitive to your warnings and obedient to how you'd have me respond.

*Y*ou can sometimes recognize Satan at work when you begin to feel backed into a corner. It's ironic that Satan tries to sell us the philosophy that God wants to squelch us and confine us and that, like Him, we should be able to do whatever we want. Satan promises wide-open spaces, but then he backs us into a pit.

If a new relationship or opportunity is causing you to feel trapped or backed into a corner, God could be flagging you that Satan is all over it. God issues dos and don'ts, but always for freedom's sake. Satan backs us into a corner on slippery ground strategically close to the nearest pit. God enlarges our steps under us, enabling us to see a pit from a greater distance so we don't have to live in constant dread of falling into another one.

Also, the fact that you are reading this book—or anything like it—betrays that Satan didn't take you anywhere near the finish line he planned for you. When you slipped into that pit, you went to a place you never intended. Now you're going to a place *Satan* never intended. Don't you stop until the enemy is sorry he ever messed with you.

What signs of Satan being at work in your life have you seen or perhaps are seeing now? Think of the psalmist's picture of God preparing a table before you in the presence of your enemy. Don't get up from that chair until God anoints you with an overflow of the Holy Spirit. Right in front of your enemy's eyes.

Lord God, I like the idea that Satan will be sorry he ever messed with me. After all, when he messes with me, he is messing with You. Thank You for being my Warrior, my Rock, my Shield.

*I am convinced that neither death nor life,
neither angels nor demons, neither the present
nor the future, nor any powers, neither height
nor depth, nor anything else in all creation,
will be able to separate us from the love
of God that is in Christ Jesus our Lord.*

Romans 8:38–39

Traps get set. Feet slip. And I hate how the enemy uses the guilt over how you got into a pit to trap you into never getting out. Hear me clearly: you cannot let him get away with that. Settle in your mind right now that staying in the pit is absolutely unacceptable. No matter how responsible and guilty you feel for sliding your way in, God wants you out. If you know Jesus Christ personally, you are not stuck. You do have the power to stand up against the enemy.

Besides, God still has a vision for you. No matter where you've been, God's full intent is for you to live effectively (John 15:8) and abundantly (John 10:10).

He loves you dearly, and the fact that you've been foolish doesn't diminish His love one single ounce. Talk to God. Echo the words of the psalmist: "If I should say, 'My foot has slipped,' Your lovingkindness, O LORD, will hold me up" (Psalm 94:18 NASB).

If you don't soak your brain in the truth that you are absolutely secure in the unchanging love of God, you will never feel worthy of getting out of the pit. Satan will keep your feet on that slippery ground.

So when you want out of your pit, you've got a golden opportunity to see the grace of God as you've never encountered it. Let God's lovingkindness hold you up.

Lord God, help me to receive, rest in, completely trust in Your love for me—and may Your love make me deaf to the enemy's false accusations about why I'm in a pit.

God does all these things to a person—
twice, even three times—
to turn them back from the pit,
that the light of life may shine on them.

Job 33:29–30

*Y*ou can jump in. That's the third and final way you can land in a pit. Before you take the plunge into that pit, you can be well aware that what you're about to do is wrong, probably even foolish. But for whatever reason, the escalating desire to do it exceeds the good sense not to. Unlike the second route into a pit, you didn't just slip in before you knew what was happening. You had time to think, and then you did exactly what you meant to do even if the pit turned out to be deeper and the consequences greater than you had expected.

When all is said and done, you—like me—probably do what you do because you want to. You ordinarily jump into a pit because you like the trip. Stay with me here, beloved. Surely you know that it takes one to know one. The only reason I'm not still in a pit is because, after many warnings, God mushroomed such devastating consequences of sin and emotional unhealthiness that it nearly killed me. God brought me to a place where I was willing to do anything to get out of the pit and everything to stay out.

Merciful God, it's humbling to cry out for deliverance—especially when I chose to jump into my pit. Thank You for getting me to this spot of humility where I am at least acknowledging that I need Your deliverance.

I love the Lord, for he heard my voice;
he heard my cry for mercy.
Because he turned his ear to me,
I will call on him as long as I live.

Psalm 116:1–2

What if you woke up today from the autopilot of poor decisions? What if a domestic tornado didn't have to huff and puff and blow your house down to get your attention? What if, before the bottom fell out, you would respond to a Voice in the wilderness saying, "Stop it!"? That Voice is very clear: "Wash and make yourselves clean. Take your evil deeds out of my sight! Stop doing wrong" (Isaiah 1:16). And what if that same Voice—the only One that matters—was willing to tell you how to stop?

That could happen. In fact, if we are willing to let it, it would happen. God in His tender mercy gives us plenty of warnings, enabling us to avoid pits, but the problem with us pit-jumpers is that we don't want to hear those warnings. We want what we want. So we stick our fingers in our ears before we jump in.

What on earth drives us to do such a thing? You've read the answer before: we want what we want. And, as sinners, we don't always want the good God wants for us.

Ears plugged, heart hardened, mind made up, lord of my own life—I know this stance way too well, Lord. Please forgive me. Please transform me.

> *The LORD searches every heart and understands every desire and every thought.*
>
> 1 Chronicles 28:9

Of all the ways into the pit, jumping in is by far the most dangerous and the most supremely *consequential*. You see, motive is huge to God. So is character. Primarily His character, which we are created to emulate. And He will not be mocked. The very segment of Scripture where we're told God won't be mocked is strategically centered in the context of reaping what we sow (Galatians 6:7–9). We can't fool Him by hiding our inner motive. God looks intently not only at what we've done and how, but also at *why* we did it. The Bible tells us that, unlike people, God doesn't look on the outward appearance of things. He looks upon the heart (1 Chronicles 28:9).

And do you want to hear something ironic? This very aspect of God (His omniscience) that helps save our scrawny necks when we've slipped into a pit (we didn't mean to) nearly hangs us when we've jumped into it (we did mean to, no matter what story we're telling). If you've ever made that jump, I really don't have to tell you that you had your reasons. You did it because of something you wanted.

It is truly amazing that we can call God "Father"; it is truly appropriate that He would call us children. Willful, selfish children even. Especially when we insist on doing what we want to do when we want to do it!

It's humbling, Lord, that You know my heart better than I know it . . . and that You love me anyway. Thank You.

> *Keep Your servant from willful sins;*
> *do not let them rule over me.*
> *Then I will be innocent*
> *and cleansed from blatant rebellion.*
>
> Psalm 19:13 HCSB

*C*an you relate to the psalmist's words? *Willful sins. Blatant rebellion.* The two are as tied together as a bird and a feather. Innate in every act of rebellion is an authority figure we're rebelling against. Hence, my hunch that if you—like the old me—keep choosing the left turn over and over again, you've got an authority problem. I know I did. We're desperate to ask God to help us overcome it. Even after we do, you and I are never going to be able to submit to authority perfection as long as our feet of clay are stuck to Planet Earth.

But don't let anybody—particularly someone touting a twisted doctrine of grace—talk you into thinking you can't be liberated from willful sin and blatant rebellion just because he or she hasn't been. I know for a fact that you can be completely set free from every sin that rules over you. Then and only then will you and I possess the kind of innocence possible for Homo sapiens still inhaling terrestrial air.

What may be contributing to your struggle to submit to authority? Now tell me what you think about this statement: "You can be completely set free from every sin that rules over you."

Lord, You know my heart, and You also know my struggle to submit to You. And I know that only You can set me free from that struggle and from every other stronghold that rules over me. Help me cooperate with that work You want to do in me.

Okay, confessions about my pit-jumping: I have often ended up doing exactly what I set out to do . . . what, at that moment or in that season, I thought I *wanted* to do. Like you, perhaps, I have wished I didn't want the things I did. I often hated what I wanted. Still, desire—deformed and destructive—lurched and led.

I had thought of my heart as only sinful. I didn't realize that deeper still, underneath that soil, my heart was sick. One of the most important shifts in my belief system began with the realization that I had a messed up "want to." My desires were tremendously unhealthy. Self-destructive. Never minimize the power of desire.

Doing what you need to do is the place to start, but

we'll never make it over the long haul motivated by need alone. The most self-disciplined among us may walk in victory for a few weeks out of the need to do the right thing, but that need will rarely carry us to the finish line. Each of us will ultimately do what we want to do.

If you have the same tendency toward pit-jumping that I do, I wish more than anything to talk you into crying out for deliverance before your world comes tumbling down. Praise God, He is the rebuilder of ruins, but surely there are easier ways to get a new home than to let an emotional tornado tear the old one to pieces.

Lord, please help me accept the truth about my heart so that I may yield it to You—the only One who can fix my messed up "want to"—before an emotional tornado strikes.

> *"In this world you will have trouble. But take heart! I have overcome the world."*
>
> Jesus in John 16:33

I am not the only one with deformed desires. I have a good friend who invited me into her harrowingly self-destructive mind. Self-destruction was my thing, too, but her emotional elevator plunged her to an even lower floor. After spending ninety days in jail for a second DUI, she expressed to me that the whole time she was there, she never had any other plan than to walk out that door and get a drink. She reasoned that the only thing she needed to do differently was perhaps not drive.

After getting out she got too drunk to keep her appointments with her probation officer and ended up spending another gig behind bars, this time for six months. A few days after release? Same thing.

In light of all she'd lost—job, marriage, kids,

self-respect—her walking out the door and doing the same thing again baffled me. I asked her why she had done it. Hadn't the relentless demand of her addicted internal organs finally had time to die down? She said dryly, "Because I wanted to. Beth, I don't think you're listening. I wanted to drink. I liked how it made me feel."

Or how it made her *not* feel.

Which of your own experiences come to mind when you read the words "Because I wanted to"? What lesson did you learn—or perhaps are you still learning—from that decision and its consequences? Focus especially on the good God is bringing out of it.

Lord God, You know when I feel overcome by the world, when the troubles seem insurmountable, when I don't want to feel anything. At those times, help me believe that You have indeed overcome the world with its sin, loss, struggles, and pain.

> *You have lovingly delivered my soul*
> *from the pit of corruption.*
>
> Isaiah 38:17 NKJV

eformed desires. The desire to *not* desire is one of the most deformed desires we'll ever have. One of the biggest mistakes we could ever make is to assume that passionate desire is wrong and that the goal for godly people is to not feel. Nothing could be further from the truth. We were created out of holy passion *for* holy passion. So perfectly fitted for passion are we that we will find it one way or another. If we don't find it in Christ, we'll find it in things like lust, anger, rage, and greed.

As I cautioned earlier, never minimize the power of desire. Each of us will ultimately do what we want to do. Is it any wonder, then, that the first words of Christ recorded in the incomparable gospel of John are "What do you want?" Hear Him echo the same words to you today: "What do you want, child?" What are your secret desires? Place them before Him. Name every single one. No matter how healthy or unhealthy. No matter how respectable. No matter how deformed. I am proof that God can heal the most messed up "want to."

God healed my deformed desires, and He can heal yours.

Lord, I ask You to fix, overhaul, heal my "want to." Show me how to cooperate with You in the process that I may choose Your way rather than any pits I find myself walking near.

*I will give you a new heart and put a new spirit
in you; I will remove from you your heart of
stone and give you a heart of flesh. And I will
put my Spirit in you and move you to follow
my decrees and be careful to keep my laws.*

Ezekiel 36:26–27

*I*n recent years no verse has meant more to me than
Psalm 40:8—"I delight to do Your will, O my God;
Your Law is within my heart" (NASB). I still can hardly
fathom that I can say those words and mean them after
where I've been.

God healed my deformed desires, finally getting
through my thick skull that the things He wanted for
me were the best things life could offer. Using the hammer of His Word and the anvil of His unfailing love,
God reshaped my disfigured desires until what I wanted
more than anything on earth was what He wanted.
Somewhere along the way, God's law transferred from
the stone tablets of my head to the soft tissue of my

heart. I bought in—not just spiritually, but emotionally. Jesus finally, completely, won my heart. And not just mine. Remember that good friend I told you about who wanted that next drink regardless of the consequences? I've never known anyone in more bondage. Christ finally got through to her, won her heart, and changed her desires. She's a miracle. I'm a miracle. And if God can deliver the two of us, He can deliver anyone.

Thank You for the deliverance and newness of heart You have already blessed me with, Lord. In faith I thank You for the deliverance and renewal You will continue to do in my life as well as the Spirit-empowered obedience You will enable.

*Now the serpent was more crafty than any of the wild animals the L*ORD *God had made. He said to the woman, "Did God really say, 'You must not eat from any tree in the garden'?" The woman said to the serpent, "We may eat fruit from the trees in the garden, but God did say, 'You must not eat fruit from the tree that is in the middle of the garden, and you must not touch it, or you will die.'" "You will not certainly die," the serpent said to the woman. "For God knows that when you eat from it your eyes will be opened, and you will be like God, knowing good and evil."*

Genesis 3:1–5

So much of our propensity toward pit-jumping springs from the fact that somewhere down deep inside, we just don't trust God. We think He's like all the others who have cheated or betrayed us. As my friend Chris Thom says, "God is not just a big us."

Like Adam and Eve, we let the enemy taunt us into believing God is holding out on us. Our drive for the proverbial forbidden fruit is our innate belief that what we are denied is exactly what we want most, what we need most, and what will make us happiest.

Satan was a liar then, and he's a liar now. When I say, "If God can deliver me, He can deliver anyone," Satan may be saying to you, "Not true!" When you hear that kind of whispering, remind yourself that Satan has always been a liar.

Forgive me, Lord God, for the ways I think of you as "a big us." Forgive me for choosing to believe Satan's lies rather than Your truth . . . You know that I want to trust You more than I do.

> *Taste and see that the LORD is good.*
>
> Psalm 34:8

*I*n my research for this book, I learned that certain kinds of relationships and people become automatic pits for us the second we intimately engage. For instance, Proverbs 22:14 warns, "The mouth of forbidden women is a deep pit" (ESV). The same is true of forbidden men. A relationship that is so enticing to us precisely because it's forbidden is nothing but a decoratively painted door to a cavernous pit. Scripture could not paint a more vivid picture: their very mouths are deep pits. Place your mouth on one of those and you kiss your solid ground good-bye.

God doesn't just say no because it makes Him feel good about Himself. God feels fine about Himself. He doesn't need us to feel small so He can feel big. He's huge. He doesn't have to be bossy to feel like the boss. He's the Master of the universe. If God forbids something, the sooner we believe and confess that He is doing so for our sakes, the better off we are.

What command are you currently struggling to obey? God already knows, so it's time for you to acknowledge the battle so you can fight it more effectively.

God's nos are for your own good. Say that out loud ten times—and believe it!

Lord, You know our human nature all too well. Someone says no, and we want forbidden territory even more passionately than before. Please work in my heart and remove that weakness in me. Help me to stop pushing back against Your nos and, instead, embrace the truth that they're for my good.

Whoever digs a pit will fall into it;
if someone rolls a stone, it
will roll back on them.

Proverbs 26:27

*P*roverbs 23:27 adds this to our discussion of forbidden relationships: "A prostitute is a deep pit; an adulteress is a narrow well" (ESV). The King James Version uses a far stronger word than *prostitute*—stronger even than the American Standard Version's *harlot*—and one that suggests that the term isn't limited to someone who is paid to have sex. It refers to anyone who sleeps around and practices immorality as a lifestyle. Needless to say, the verse is equally true in gender reversal. A man who sleeps around is a deep pit, and an adulterer is a narrow well. Mess with them and, in a manner of speaking, you'll hurl yourself into the bowels of the earth with such meteoric force that only God can pull you out.

I don't care how flattering someone's attention may be. If he or she is immoral or married to somebody else, an intimate relationship of any kind with that person will automatically—not probably or eventually—hurl you into a pit. ETA? Instantaneously.

Disobeying God's commands may begin on a sweet high, but will inevitably turn sour and unpleasant. Entering into forbidden relationships is no exception.

Lord, You created cause and effect, and You are clear in Your Word about actions and consequences. Thank You for the warnings in Your Word—and thank You for Your Spirit who can help me not only hear Your warnings but also walk according to Your will.

*No matter how many promises God
has made, they are "Yes" in Christ.*

2 Corinthians 1:20

*B*ased on everything the Word of God says and everything I've experienced, heard, or observed, I promise you that forbidden relationships never turn out well. Let me say that one more time: *never*. The pit is deep and dark. And before you know it, you'll find that you are in it all alone.

I've also lived long enough and listened hard enough to become convinced that we are almost always right, no matter how much we don't want to be, when we get a nagging feeling somewhere down inside that a person to whom we're growing increasingly attached has a serious dark side. That's the Holy Spirit warning us. Learn to associate darkness with a pit. I say all of this to you out of deep love and concern. Repent and run.

One more thing. Keep in mind that automatic pit-jumping can be circumstantial and relational and that it is prompted by a far broader range of behaviors and attitudes than matters of sexuality. Forbidden sexual relationships simply trigger some of God's boldest guarantees of disaster. The wider context is that anything God goes to the trouble to forbid can mean automatic pit-dwelling.

He's actually a yes kind of God. But you can mark this one down any time and every time . . . 24/7 . . . 365 days of the year: God's no is a quick shove away from a pit. The sooner the shove, the better.

Gracious Lord God, thank you for loving me enough to say no whenever I need to hear it. Please help me recognize and be sensitive to the leading of Your voice. Make my desire be to put myself and my harmful ways aside, and turn to You and Your ways, which are always good.

My son, if sinful men entice you,
do not give in to them. . . .
Do not go along with them,
do not set foot on their paths;
for their feet rush into evil,
they are swift to shed blood.

Proverbs 1:10, 15–16

I don't want you to get the wrong idea, so let me clarify: I didn't begin to live in victory just because all opportunity to jump finally disappeared. That's not the case at all. While I was still at greatest risk, God stayed on me, worked with me, and built trust in me until finally I'd go where He pointed. That's been our—God's and my—MO for a while now, but He's wise to never let me forget the excruciating pain of where I've been . . . lest I be tempted to go back. Until we're nine-tenths in the grave, none of us is past the danger of a pit.

Get a load of the words out of King David's mouth immediately after promising God he'd lead a blameless life: "When will you come to me?" (Psalm 101:2 NIV).

David is saying, "I don't know how long I can keep this up. Are you coming soon? Killing me soon?" And can't we pit-jumpers relate? Quick carnal impulses leap into all of our heads at times, but once we've let God win our hearts, a high tide of holy desire can come and wash them away like jellyfish swept from the shore.

What has kept God from completely winning your heart? What is in the way right now?

I can't encourage you enough, beloved: let God win your heart so you can stand strong.

Lord, it is crazy the way those carnal impulses intrude and entice. When that happens, I want to turn to You, be strong in You, and experience Your filling me with a high tide of holy desire.

*When tempted, no one should say, "God is
tempting me." For God cannot be tempted
by evil, nor does he tempt anyone; but each
person is tempted when they are dragged
away by their own evil desire and enticed.*

James 1:13–14

*I*t's a long story, but I once talked about my young
friend Savannah and the Barbies she brought to
worship, and I've been receiving Barbies ever since. A
recent Barbie I received was dressed like me (hip, I hope,
but modest). She had a makeshift Bible in one hand
while the other was stretched decisively heavenward.
This doll had one inadvertent similarity to me that
overrode all the others. One of Barbie's feet had been
gnawed right off at the calf. The group extended their
regrets, of course, explaining that the family dog of the
original owner had gotten hold of the doll the day before
they left. They were disappointed but decided the doll
was, by and large, no worse for the wear.

I stared at the Barbie for a minute. She looked so

strange at first. So well coiffed, and yet she had a gnawed-off foot. Then I nodded. Not to anyone else really. Just to God. Though the group didn't know it, they'd hit the nail right on the head. That was me all right.

No, I don't have a missing leg, but if you could see me with your spiritual eyes, surely at least one of my legs is gnawed off at the knee. Satan has wounded me, but he hasn't devoured me. I may walk with a spiritual limp, but thanks be to God, who holds me up and urges me to lean on Him, at least I can walk. So can you. Walk away from that pit—even with a limp—before it's the death of you.

Thank You, Lord, for spiritual limps that keep us mindful of our need for You—for Your strength and guidance, hope and love.

I can do all this through him
who gives me strength.

Philippians 4:13

*Y*ou can get out. Regardless of whether you were thrown in, you slipped in, or you jumped in, you can get out of your pit. And I do mean *you*. I'm not talking about the person who seems to deal with her pit better than you do. We don't need to deal with our pits. We need to get out of our pits. You can do it. Even if you have a history of failed attempts. Even if you don't think you deserve it. Even if you've never lived anywhere else.

But here's the catch: you can't get yourself out. Try as you may, you will never successfully pull yourself out of a pit. Not the kind the Word of God is talking about. Remember the number one characteristic of a pit? Mud and mire. The quicksand kind that gulps your feet whole. You're stuck. As much as you'd like to, as self-sufficient as you'd like to be, as smug as it would make you, you can't do this one alone. Somebody else has to come to your rescue. But there you have options. You can opt for human help or you can opt for God.

As with any choice, the options of human help and God's help have their advantages and disadvantages. Carefully consider when the advantages outweigh the disadvantages.

Lord, You know how appealing it is for me to act in my own strength. And You know the smugness that results when I think I succeed. But You also know how deep and sticky this pit's mud is and how much I need You to be my Deliverer. Show me how to accept Your offer in the day-to-day and not just mentally acquiesce and deceive myself.

The Lord is my rock, my fortress
and my deliverer;
my God is my rock, in whom I take refuge,
my shield and the horn of my
salvation, my stronghold.

Psalm 18:2

Okay, you're in a pit. You can get out. You *can* get out—and *you* can get out. But you can't do this one alone. Somebody else has to come to your rescue. And you have a choice. You can opt for human help or you can opt for God.

To actually see our deliverer could be a decisive advantage. To have an audible conversation would be great. To know that someone really was listening would help. To see the look on a face or hear the tone in voice—now, to us, that would be a real help.

But help alone is not what we're talking about. God meant for people to offer one another a helping hand. The trouble comes when we insist upon someone who is as human as we are becoming our deliverer. Another person—rare though he may be—can pull us out of a pit, but—for the life of him—he can't set us free.

What source of help are you opting for? Human help whom you can see, be hugged by, and have an audible conversation with—or God's help, which is limitless and perfect in wisdom and love?

Lord God, You know I can answer with my words that I'm seeking Your help, but my actions may not reflect that. Enable me to choose You as my helper even as I accept Your help through Your people.

I lift up my eyes to the mountains—
where does my help come from?
My help comes from the LORD,
the Maker of heaven and earth.

Psalm 121:1–2

*D*id you realize that the first time Scripture mentions a pit, Joseph was in it? While he was kicking and screaming in the waterless bottom, his brothers looked up from their picnic lunch and saw a camel caravan on its way to Egypt. Judah had the great idea of selling Joseph rather than killing him. After all, Judah said, "He is our brother, our own flesh and blood" (Genesis 37:27). So his brothers pulled Joseph out of the pit and sold him to the travelers.

Agreed, getting sold into slavery was a far better option than starving to death in the bottom of the cistern. But a kind soul will give the brothers too much credit for their compassion without Psalm 105:18 to round out the picture. We're told that the Ishmaelites "bruised his feet with shackles, his neck was put in irons." Don't forget, Joseph was only seventeen. Pampered and spoiled at that. Suddenly, at the drop of a head wrap, he was a slave in shackles.

Scripture leaves no doubt that the sovereignty of God was in full pendulum swing, directing every detail from Canaan to Egypt for the common good. Years passed, however, before Joseph began to grasp the work of his true Deliverer.

Think back to a time when you opted for human help rather than God's. In what ways was that help at least better than, figuratively speaking, starving to death at the bottom of your pit?

Lord, You understand better than I that even when people have helped me out of a pit, I still very much needed a Deliverer. Help me never settle for physical deliverance from a pit when You want so much more for me.

God's sovereign hand was definitely behind the business transaction—a deal made at Joseph's great expense—between Joseph's brothers and the Midianite merchants. Years passed, however, before Joseph the slave began to grasp the work that God, his true Deliverer, was doing. In our relational parallel, if a man—or woman—pulls us out of the pit, solely assuming the role of deliverer, he or she will inadvertently sell us into slavery of one kind or another every time.

Scripture records several instances when God heard the cries of His people and raised up a human deliverer for them instead of insisting, as He did at other times, that they look to Him alone. Each time, Israel invariably returned to captivity. Psalm 78 chronicles a disturbing record of Israel's cycle of defeat: "In spite of [God's] wonders, they did not believe. So he ended their days in futility" (vv. 32, 33).

Here's the important part: "They did not believe in God or trust *his deliverance*" (v. 22, emphasis mine). Though God raised up leaders like Moses and Joshua, the nation still eventually defaulted to its old pattern.

What makes us default to our old patterns despite tangible evidence of God's faithfulness? Those old patterns can be exhausting. God offers us rest from it—rest for our souls—when we turn to Him in trust.

Lord, as I read about Israel's pattern of trusting, straying, trusting, straying, I realize that their pattern is mine as well. Forgive me for ways I am turning from You even today . . . and help me trust You more.

"Woe to the obstinate children,"
declares the LORD,
"to those who carry out plans that are not mine,
forming an alliance, but not by my Spirit,
heaping sin upon sin . . .
everyone will be put to shame
because of a people useless to them."

Isaiah 30:1, 5

*Y*es, the nation of Israel defaulted to its old pattern of independence from God. I know the feeling. I have had a few great leaders along the way, too, but they couldn't rewire my hard drive. I'd eventually default every time. Nothing is more futile or leaves us more fractured than trusting man to be our god. Sometimes we forget what a mistake this was the last time we did it. Time has a way of distorting our memories. That's what happened to Israel.

Not many years after the writer of Psalm 78 put pen to parchment, Israel found herself scrambling for help as she faced imminent takeover by the massive army of the Assyrians. God could have thwarted the assault in a blink of His holy eye, but He stayed His hand, awaiting their cry of repentance.

Yet, rather than humble themselves and do what was required for true protection and restoration, Israel preferred calling upon the Egyptians for protection. (Been there too.) While history etched a stark warning, they slapped a coat of gloss over their past and decided Egypt wasn't all that bad. Particularly when compared to the threatening Assyrians. They figured they'd align with Egypt and she would deliver them . . .

Of course, God could deliver us without your even asking Him, but more often than not He waits for us to approach Him, softened, repentant, and willing to let Him be Lord.

Show me, Lord, where I am trusting man to be my god, not You. And sharpen my memory, that I may recall not only the consequences of my independence from You but, more importantly, Your great faithfulness to me.

> *The Lord is the everlasting God,*
> *the Creator of the ends of the earth.*
> *He will not grow tired or weary,*
> *and his understanding no one can fathom.*
> *He gives strength to the weary*
> *and increases the power of the weak.*
>
> Isaiah 40:28–29

*I*srael didn't need Egypt. She needed God. At his best, man can make a mighty fine man, but he's a useless god. Contrary to the serpent's suggestion in the Garden, people simply can't be divine. The higher the expectation we have for them, the further they're going to fall. And somehow, when it's all over, we feel disgraced. Embarrassed. Sometimes we don't even know why.

People can help us but they can't heal us. People can lift us but they can't carry us. On occasion people can pull us out of a pit, but they cannot keep us out. Nor can they set our feet upon a rock. When we come out of a pit, if our idea of stability is standing on another human's shoulders, his clay feet will inevitably crumble, and we'll take a tumble. The job's too big for him.

In what ways or in what situation are you currently relying on another human being to be your deliverer? In what situations are you currently trying to be another person's deliverer?

Remember, a person—even you and me with our good intentions and hearts of love—is a useless god.

Almighty, all-wise, and all-loving God, You want to be Lord of our lives—when we're trying to avoid pits, when we find ourselves in a pit, and when we're crying to You to deliver us from our pit. Teach me to live with You on solid ground and as truly the Lord of my life.

*Give thanks to the Lord, for he is
good; his love endures forever.*

1 Chronicles 16:34

Since pit-dwelling is primarily a state of mind, effective deliverance also takes the ability to read people's minds, because what we say often doesn't match where we are. Only God can hang with us through the length and depth of our need. And the length and depth of our baloney. Maybe I'm just talking about myself, but whether or not I realized it, I usually found a way to frame my pit to make me look like a victim.

Not only is God omniscient, but His Word is "sharper than any double-edged sword" cutting our baloney so He can see straight through it. He knows when we're kidding others. He knows when we're kidding ourselves. Knowing all we are, all we feel, and all we hide, God overflows with love and willingness to deliver us. Even after Israel sought the help of the Egyptians, inviting the chastisement of God, the prophet Isaiah testified, "The LORD longs to be gracious to you; therefore he will rise up to show you compassion" (Isaiah 30:18).

Think of a time from your own life that comes to mind when you think about God's great compassion toward you—and thank Him for that.

The Lord truly does long to be gracious to us. Camp on that thought for a while.

Lord, thanks for reminding me that Your cutting through my baloney is an act of love and deliverance on Your part. I don't always—or maybe ever—appreciate that love in the moment, but I am choosing to believe that, perfect Father, You are working in my life and my heart for my own good.

> *He who began a good work in you will carry it on to completion until the day of Christ Jesus.*
>
> Philippians 1:6

*I*saiah 30:18 is definitely worth revisiting: "The LORD longs to be gracious to you; therefore he will rise up to show you compassion." *Longs to be gracious.* I like the ring of that.

We're also repeatedly told in Scripture that "His love endures forever," which means the Lord is gracious for a long time. That's what former pit-dwellers like me must have. We need a Deliverer who is in for the long haul.

Philippians 1:6 tells us that God, who began a good work, is faithful to complete it. Frankly, work doesn't get harder than pit-dweller pulling. Man, who may begin a good work, wears out too fast to finish it. And rightly he should. It's not his job. True delivery takes some time, some titanic effort, and more patience than the best of people possess. You and I need a strong arm and a long arm.

The apostle Paul aptly described God's tenacity in 2 Corinthians 1:10 when he said, "He *has* delivered us . . . he *will* deliver us again. On him we have set our hope that he will *continue* to deliver us" (emphasis mine). Past. Present. Future. That's exactly the kind of deliverance from the pit you and I are looking for.

God's graciousness, His love, the good work He is doing in you, His deliverance—you can count on all these every minute of your life, 24/7, for as long as you live.

Lord, it's sheer craziness that I turn away from You, fail to call on You, and struggle to trust You when You are all about being gracious and loving, when You are doing in me a good work of deliverance and transformation into Christlikeness. Teach me to walk more closely with You.

> *We say with confidence, "The Lord is my*
> *helper; I will not be afraid. What can mere*
> *mortals do to me?" . . . Jesus Christ is the*
> *same yesterday and today and forever.*
>
> Hebrews 13:6, 8

*G*od *has* delivered us. He *will* deliver us. And He will *continue* to deliver us. We have this promise of past, present, and future deliverance in writing in 2 Corinthians 1:10. And there's more. We've got a lifetime warranty from God Himself: the "Sovereign LORD" alone is "my strong deliverer" (Psalm 140:7). Everybody else will wear out. They may pull us out of that pit and even hang around awhile to push us away when we try to get right back in it. But eventually their backs will give out. And when they do, we're liable to be mad at them. In fact, we might not speak to them for years. They let us down . . .

Now I can relate from both sides. I'm sure I've worn

people out, and I've been worn out (we'll get to that later). A fellow human may have initially pulled us out of a pit, but somewhere along the way, he or she accidentally sold us into the slavery of nearly debilitating disappointment. Like a ravenous beast, countless relationships ultimately demand to be fed more than people have the emotional resources to give. Reasonable expectations cease to satisfy. The beast ties up both parties to a post of excessive responsibility. The ties are ordinarily too knotted and tangled to be sorted out rationally together. One person invariably cuts the rope before the other, leaving the remaining party feeling, in the words of author William Dean Howells, "betrayed and baffled still."

Well, are you ready for some good news? We can wear people out, and people can wear us out, but you and I can never wear God out!

Lord God, I get tired of my stuff! I wear myself out!
What amazing love that I will never wear You out!

$\mathcal{I}$ wouldn't for a minute minimize the pain of a relationship broken by unreasonable—or, at the very least, unsustainable—expectations. I've knelt with too many weeping women at the altar of my church sanctuary only to learn that they needed prayer over feelings deeply hurt by someone sitting elsewhere in that room. When such a close and dependable relationship is injuriously severed, the knife penetrates to the exact depth we've invited them into our private lives. Indeed, one of the primary reasons we're so wounded is because the person knew what we were going through and still abandoned us.

What I'm about to say can be painful to hear, but I pray that God will use it toward someone's healing: sometimes a person abandons us not in spite of what we're going through, but directly because of it. They either ran out of answers or they ran out of energy and no longer had the wherewithal to go through it with us. If our helping friends actually did something that overtly wronged us, they bear responsibility before God for that. But if they wronged us only by running out of fuel and dropping out of the struggle, we might need to realize they've done all they felt they could humanly do and let them go without bitterness or anger.

Our friends are only human, and our expectations for them—especially when we're hurting—can require superhuman insight and strength. No wonder they let us down. Know that Jesus won't.

Lord Jesus, we human beings can and do run out of gas. Thank You that You can't. And thank You for laying down Your life for us when we were still Your enemies so that we are now blessed to be called Your friends.

Love is patient, love is kind. It does not envy,
it does not boast, it is not proud. It does not
dishonor others, it is not self-seeking, it is not
easily angered, it keeps no record of wrongs.

1 Corinthians 13:4–5

*Y*ou and I don't want to be afraid of intimacy or shrink back from bearing our true estate with people. If we do, we'll become as cold and hard as plastic and shelve ourselves from every purpose of our existence. (For starters, inauthentic people are ineffective people. For finishers, liberty cannot exist apart from transparency.) Human clay finds its moisture in relationships and will evaporate into dust without them. The problem comes when our idea of relationships becomes ownership—when we start thinking of the person who was willing to get into our mess with us as our personal trainer.

A few particularly faithful pit-pullers may genuinely try to hang with it for a while. For months. Even years.

If they don't seem to complain much, maybe the process is feeding something unhealthy in them too. You may reason that at least they didn't sell you off into slavery. Oh yes, they did. The world has a name for this caravan: *codependency*. The only difference between the two scenarios is that, in this one, the pit-puller jumped on the wagon to Egypt with you.

In what ways do relationships give you life? If such life-giving relationships are currently sparse, where might you go to build relationships with individuals who will love, encourage, sharpen, and build you up?

Remember, authenticity and transparency are key to life-giving relationships, and life-giving relationships fueled by 1 Corinthians 13 love are key to authenticity and transparency. It's a wonderful un-vicious circle to be part of.

Almighty God, thank You for relationships characterized by Your love so that we can know life-giving, life-changing fellowship.

As iron sharpens iron,
so one person sharpens another.

Proverbs 27:17

Have you noticed that we sometimes latch onto someone for dear life who is no better off than we are? I believe strongly in support groups, but a support group alone will never get us out of a pit. Somebody in that group better be on the upside looking in. Preferably way up. Otherwise we're liable to keep cheering back and forth, "That was so good!" when, in reality, none of us is doing well. If we keep patting each other on our broken backs, how will they ever mend? Christ asked the question more effectively in Luke 6:39: "Can the blind guide the blind? Shall they not both fall into a pit?" (ASV).

Now let's switch sides for a minute. Not only has each of us searched for a human deliverer, we've also tried to become a deliverer to someone else. I could offer an embarrassing number of personal examples, but suffice it to say my experiences have settled something for me: even if we are unselfish and undistracted enough to give another person our all for an indefinite period of time, can we save them from themselves? I don't think so.

Does this mean we should not get involved with hurting people? Not at all! We may be hopelessly inadequate as deliverers for one another, but never think for a moment we can't be used of God to affect profound change in someone's life.

God can and does use us in the lives of other people. That's the primary reason He leaves us here on Planet Earth after our citizenship has transferred to heaven.

Lord, please use me in people's lives as You will—to be iron sharpening iron, to affect profound change for their good, but not to be their deliverer. In fact, please keep me from ever trying to take on that role!

> *Two are better than one . . . If either*
> *of them falls down, one can help the*
> *other up. But pity anyone who falls*
> *and has no one to help them up.*
>
> Ecclesiastes 4:9–10

We can have a tremendous impact over a life in the pit. First of all, we can impact pit-dwellers by example. We can show them that living outside the pit is possible by living that way ourselves. If living outside of pits is impossible, the whole concept remains celebratory theology at best and pitifully poor reality.

Second, we can impact pit-dwellers by prayer. Second Corinthians 1:10–11 says this: "on [God] we have set our hope that he will continue to deliver us, as *you help us by your prayers*" (emphasis mine). We have a God-given invitation—if not responsibility—to join the process of someone's divine deliverance from peril or pit. When deliverance happens, the payoff is glorious.

Third, we can impact pit-dwellers by encouragement. Hebrews 3:13 calls us to "encourage one another daily . . . that none of you may be hardened by sin's deceitfulness." Satan has a tremendous investment in convincing a person that, with his or her track record, sustainable victory is impossible. That's a lie. Say so.

Lord Jesus, You gave me an example of how to live outside a pit in rich fellowship with and life-giving dependency on God. You are at His right hand praying for me. You have given Your Holy Spirit as my Comforter, Counselor, and Encourager.

The fear of the LORD is the beginning of wisdom.

Psalm 111:10

We can definitely be used of God to affect profound change in someone's life. Our example, our prayer, and our encouragement are three ways.

Fourth, we can impact pit-dwellers by doggedly directing them to Jesus. Like the men carrying the paralytic on the mat, do everything you can to "lay [the person] before Jesus" (Luke 5:18). All the while keep praying, encouraging, and living by example. And above all, keep telling that person who the true Deliverer is. Keep pointing her toward the only One who will not let her down.

Fifth, to the degree that God has developed biblical wisdom in us, we can impact pit-dwellers through our advice and counsel. I am a huge proponent of godly professional counseling. Got it myself, and I'm not sure where I'd be without it. When someone brings me an issue way out of my league, I'm going to stay on her like a bird dog on point until she goes to counseling.

When has God spoken His wisdom through one of His people at just the time you needed that word of guidance, encouragement, chastisement, or hope from Him? When you have the opportunity to be that kind of truth-speaker, what role does prayer play in your offer of biblical wisdom?

Our example, our prayer, our encouragement, our pointing people to Jesus, and our advice or counsel—which may be advising the pit-dweller to find professional counseling—are ways God can use us to bring healing change to the life of someone He cares about.

Here am I, Lord! At the right time, I pray, use me as an agent of Your hope and Your healing. And, Lord, when I am in need, I ask You to provide me with such people in my life.

> *"Turn to me and be saved,*
> *all you ends of the earth;*
> *for I am God, and there is no other."*
>
> Isaiah 45:22

*A*ll of us were born with a natural tendency to attach ourselves to a savior and worship him. To see him high and lifted up. That's why it had better be Christ. We are safe with no other. Isaiah 43:11 says it succinctly: "I, even I, am the LORD, and apart from me there is no savior."

No one else can handle the weight. They may try for a while. They may even like it for a while, because when someone looks up to you and depends on you, it can be heady. But sooner or later they will drop the rope. It's too much to carry. Like the men who lowered the paralytic through the roof of the home where Jesus was teaching, you finally have to let go of the rope and leave that person in need with Jesus.

And maybe someone has finally had to leave you with Jesus. Maybe you were left disillusioned or disappointed when that person dropped the rope. Possibly devastated. But maybe now you're beginning to see that this person wasn't being heartless and hateful. Maybe you can now forgive yourself for accidentally setting someone up for failure. And maybe both of you—and me too—could just let Jesus be Jesus.

Lord, help me be thankful for people You send to help me, but keep me from making them a savior. Teach me, I ask, to let Jesus be Jesus—to let Him be my Deliverer and my Lord—in every aspect of my life.

> *"My grace is sufficient for you, for my power is made perfect in weakness."*
>
> God to the apostle Paul in
> 2 Corinthians 12:9

*Y*ou can opt for God. Pitching every other plan, you can opt for God. Thanks-but-no-thanks to every other deliverer, you can opt for God. Not just for His help, but for His entire Person! The whole of God.

You can opt for the *Father* who reigns as King over every intricate detail in the universe and can micromanage a complicated life like yours and mine. You can opt for the *Son* who paid your debt in full, not just to deliver you from earth to heaven when you die, but also from pit to pavement while you live. I don't care what kind of addiction you've had or what kind of places you've been, you have as much right to flourish in Christ's abundance as Billy Graham. And you can opt for the *Holy Spirit* who first hovered over the Genesis waters and brought order out of chaos.

The beautiful thing about opting for God is that you are opting for everything He brings. Because He is infinite, you will never reach the end of all He offers of Himself. Nothing on earth is like fully engaging with God. *Nothing.* God's love is better than life. No one compares.

Reflect on a moment when you experienced, or at least glimpsed, the truth that God's love is better than life.

Lord, I can identify moments of rebellion and dis-obedience, but I am undoubtedly unaware of the many ways I subtly choose other than You in the course of my day. Teach me, by Your grace, to choose You in all that I think, do, and say.

You are worthy, our Lord and God, to receive glory and honor and power, for you created all things, and by your will they were created and have their being.

Revelation 4:11

If you're willing to engage God as your Deliverer from the pit, the full-throttle relationship you develop with Him will be the most glorious thing that has ever happened to you. Far more glorious than the deliverance itself. If you will take God up on what He offers so that you can live in victory, you will find thankfulness in your heart for every person who let you down. For ultimately, their failure set you up for the most ecstatic relationship you will ever experience.

If you're willing. Here comes the challenge, and if you decide to take the challenge, beloved, you are on your way out of that pit. Here's the deal: God wants everything you've got. Uncontested priority. Every egg in one basket. All your weight on one limb. This very moment

He has His fingers gripped on your chin, saying, "Right here, Child. Look right here. Don't look right or left. Stare straight into My face. I am your Deliverer. There is none like Me."

God will be your complete Deliverer—or nothing at all. That's the one rule of divine rescue. God absolutely refuses to share His glory. God may use any number of people in your life—friends, a counselor, a family member, or fellow believers—to come alongside and encourage as part of His process. But He alone must deliver you . . . . or you will never be free.

Show me, Lord, where else I am looking for deliverance and who else I am turning to as my deliverer. Help me look right into Your face and wholeheartedly accept Your offer to be my Deliverer.

Yes, my soul, find rest in God;
my hope comes from him.
Truly he is my rock and my salvation;
he is my fortress, I will not be shaken.
My salvation and my honor depend on God;
he is my mighty rock, my refuge.

Psalm 62:5–7

Too many of our American churches never even tackle issues of sin, addiction, and defeat. You can get such a steady dose of "feel good" sermons that you actually start to feel pretty good about that pit you're in. That's not the goal. Soothing words can become just another drug we swallow to dull our pain. Other Christian environments that actually do exercise the courage to call sin a sin can sometimes be tiresomely long-winded on what's wrong with us and pitifully short on what to do about it.

Picture attending a weekly weight-loss meeting and hearing, "You're too fat!" echoed throughout most of the session, followed by a succinct two-word wrap-up:

"Lose weight!" You'd leave really encouraged, wouldn't you? Empowered for the task? Instead, and to their credit, countless weight-loss groups actually equip their participants for success, with victors candidly sharing what they discovered and those still in defeat standing on their tiptoes in a little ray of hope.

We Christians hold in our hands the incomparable manual for life, bulging with instructions, reasons, and countless real, human examples to illustrate them. So why are we getting shown up all over the place?

Lord God, as it comes time to take steps toward the total deliverance You alone offer me, please give me strength and courage to take those steps.

> *[May you know] his incomparably great power for us who believe. That power is the same as the mighty strength he exerted when he raised Christ from the dead.*
>
> Ephesians 1:19–20

Why are we believers who own—I'm just guessing here—at least a couple versions of God's Guide to Life not finding in those pages of Scripture the Path to deliverance and why are we not getting to know the Deliverer better?

Many of us in sterner Christian circles have substitut ed equipping and getting equipped for weekly poundings: "You're too _____! Lose _____!" And they're probably right; we are too prideful, selfish, worldly, lustful, or whatever. And we do need to lose the root cause of those sins. But how do we lose it? We don't even know how we found it!

If we're really convicted, we drag ourselves to the altar

and tell God how sorry we are . . . *again*. And we are sorry. We're miserable. We know something has to change, but we've got so many issues, we don't know where to start. We don't even know who we are without them.

Still, we keep coming back to church because we figure we deserve, if not hell, at least a weekly beating. I don't mean to sound cynical. I love the body of Christ deeply and I love church. But I'm jealous for the tens of thousands, maybe more, who still make their bed in a pit. Not one of us has to be left there. Every one of us who authentically calls Jesus "Lord" has the right and power to be victorious.

If you call Jesus your Savior and Lord, may He use my offering of His truth in these pages to give you hope.

Lord, in You I have the power to be victorious over all that leads me into a pit. Teach me to access and live in the resurrection power You make available to Your children through Your Spirit.

*I waited patiently for the L*ORD*;*
he turned to me and heard my cry.
He lifted me out of the slimy pit,
out of the mud and mire;
he set my feet on a rock
and gave me a firm place to stand.

Psalm 40:1–2

Having established that one unwavering rule—God will be your complete Deliverer, or nothing at all—let's get busy. To get where we want to go, we need a comprehendible, biblical how-to. We need lasting answers that don't just target our behaviors. We need answers that tap the power of heaven and change the thoughts and feelings that drive those behaviors. And this is my offering . . .

I believe the Bible proposes three steps for getting out of the pit:

Cry out
Confess
Consent

We'll take a look at each step.

In Psalm 40:1–2, the pit-dweller's deliverance began with a cry. I'm not talking about tears. Yes, weeping may accompany this cry, but tears alone mean little. We can cry our eyes out over the pain of our situation and still refuse to change. Those kinds of tears often flow from our desperation for *God* to change and our frustration that He won't. If you're like me, sometimes you want Him to bend the rules for you and bless your disobedience or half-heartedness.

His refusal to bend to our will may at first seem uncompassionate in light of all we've endured, but He's pushing for the best thing that will ever happen to us. He will never pat your broken back and say, "Who could blame you for all of this?" God wants you up on your feet, living abundantly, profoundly, effectively.

Lord, in my view from the pit, it's hard to imagine what living abundantly would look like, but I'm willing to give it a shot. Help me cooperate with Your efforts to lift me "out of the slimy pit" and give me "a firm place to stand."

I love the LORD, for he heard my voice;
he heard my cry for mercy.
Because he turned his ear to me,
I will call on him as long as I live.

Psalm 116:1–2

God wants you up on your feet, living abundantly, profoundly, effectively—and it all begins with a cry that erupts from the deepest part of your soul as if your life depends on it. This cry from the depths of the pit is aimed straight up those narrow walls to the throne of God. No random ear will do for this kind of crier. He is aiming at the One who made all things, rules all things, and can change all things. The One who says nothing is impossible. You will be hard pressed to find a more repetitive concept in Scripture than God's intervention coming as a direct response to someone crying out. Psalm 116:1–2 is just a sample.

Why does the process start with our cry? Why can't it just begin with our need? I mean, God is all knowing for heaven's sake. He knows what we need before we ask Him, so why does He make us bother? Mind you, God can do whatever He wants. He can run to the rescue of anyone, regardless of her awareness or acknowledgment of Him. No telling how many times He's done it for us and we simply never knew what trouble we avoided. However, Scripture proves that God more often waits until the challenge comes and the hurting cry out (Exodus 3:7–8).

God is sovereign and has His own reasons for responding in the ways He does. But from what I can tell about Him, I think He usually waits for us to cry out so He can remove all doubt about who came to our rescue.

Lord, You alone are worthy of glory. So when my deliverance comes, may I give You and You alone the glory. And as You teach me to live abundantly, may that glory-giving continue.

My mouth will tell of your righteous deeds,
of your saving acts all day long . . .
I will come and proclaim your mighty acts,
Sovereign Lord;
I will proclaim your righteous
deeds, yours alone. . . .
to this day I declare your marvelous deeds.

Psalm 71:15–17

*D*id you hear me? (What mom or dad hasn't said that?) I'm going to repeat myself because this truth is so important . . . .

God is sovereign, and He has His own reasons for responding in the ways He does. But from what I can tell about Him, I think He usually waits for us to cry out so He can remove all doubt about who came to our rescue. We need to expand this idea.

You see, if we never cried out and if we had no human to credit when the raging fires of our trials turned to embers, we'd likely chalk our deliverance up to circumstantial happenstance or saccharine philosophies like "Things have a way of working out, don't they?" Things don't just work out. God works them out. Blessed is the one who knows it.

Further, God sees great advantage in awaiting our cry because He is unequivocally driven by relationship. Throughout your ascent out of that pit, never lose sight of the fact that God will forever be more interested in you knowing your Healer than in you experiencing His healing, and more interested in you knowing your Deliverer than in you knowing your deliverance. The King of all creation wants to reveal Himself to you. His Highness is willing to come to us in our lowness. Our cries blow the lid off the cistern we're trapped in. They voice openness. Readiness. That's what God is after.

Again, *things* don't just work out. *God* works them out. When have you seen God clearly come to the rescue and work out a situation for you or someone you know?

Lord God, please give me eyes to see Your hand in the circumstances of my life—Your hand of deliverance, protection, guidance, healing, and love—that I may live with a heart of gratitude.

> *"Come to me . . . and I will give you rest.*
> *Take my yoke upon you and learn from*
> *me, for I am gentle and humble in heart,*
> *and you will find rest for your souls. For*
> *my yoke is easy and my burden is light."*
>
> Jesus in Matthew 11:28–30

*H*is people's openness to Him. Our readiness for Him to work in our life and change our heart. That's what God is after.

The kind of cry that reflects such openness to the Lord can come either from the desperate "I *need* God and God alone" or the deliberate "I *want* God and God alone." Remember, we don't always have to wait until we're desperate. We can wise up enough to know how desperate we'll be if we don't cry out immediately. Either approach, regardless of how it sounds to human ears, rises to the throne of God with the volume of a foghorn in a shower stall. *Cry out.* Open your mouth, say, "God, help me!" and mean it. Not as a figure of speech.

Not with half a heart. With everything you've got, look up and cry out. Bring heaven to a standstill. Get some attention.

You can cry out loudly and demonstratively. I've done it myself. Or you can do it face down on the ground making no sound at all, except for a groan you yourself can't even interpret. However you do it, just do it. And mean it. If you don't have it, if your throat is too parched from pain and your soul is too drained of the needed energy, ask God to give you what it takes. Cry out to the one and only God who can deliver you.

Lord, through the years You've heard my desperate as well as my deliberate cries for help. You've heard the loud cries and the silent groans. Thank You that I can turn to You no matter what shape I'm in and know You will deliver me.

The LORD is near to all who call on him,
to all who call on him in truth.

Psalm 145:18

After you cry out, *confess.* Think sin, but then think wider. Though it's absolutely vital, confessing sin is not the only way we practice confession. In its widest sense, confession is our means of baring our heart and soul before God. Confession is a way we agree with what God says about Himself and about us. Confession takes place every time you tell God how much you need Him. So tell Him what's on your mind. What kind of mess you're in. Who's in it with you. What's holding you back. Who's broken your heart. Even if your first impulse is to think it's Him. As long as you can feel it, spill it.

Confession, by the way, is incomplete until we actively accept God's certain forgiveness. Take a fresh look at 1 John 1:9: "If we confess our sins, he is faithful and just and will forgive us our sins and purify us from all unrighteousness." And 1 John 3:21–22: "Dear friends, if our hearts do not condemn us, we have confidence before God and receive from him anything we ask, because we keep his commands and do what pleases him."

"If our hearts do not condemn us." Our self-condemning hearts can't block our forgiveness, but they can keep us from feeling forgiven. The result will be a twisted resignation to our own capacity to sin rather than any confidence in God's capacity to restore us.

What, if anything, keeps you from feeling forgiven by God? Talk to Him—and perhaps to a fellow believer—about it. Remember, step 1 . . . Cry out: "God, help me!" Step 2 . . . Confess: agree with what God says about Himself and about you.

Lord, in obedience to Your Word, I confess my sin . . . I confess my constant need for You . . . I share my heartache and my frustrations. And I ask You to free me from self-condemnation that I may better know the grace of Your forgiveness.

*D*on't overlook the unparalleled benefits of confessing sin. Let the light of God shine all over your sin so the two of you can sort it out and He can heal you. We will never get so hyper-spiritual that we can authentically go days upon end without anything to confess, especially considering that God places our attitudes and motives on a level with our actions.

That said, don't forget to spit out sins of pride. Nothing contributes more to the length of our stay in the pit. Pride is the number one reason why a person who knows better remains reluctant to cry out to God. In my own journey, God showed me that I'd never break the pit cycle if I didn't name every contribution I made to it and let Him deal with my self-destructive tendencies.

So even if you were thrown into your pit, search your heart to see if bitterness, anger, lack of forgiveness, or coldness has taken root. Get as specific as you can, and when you think you've thought of everything, ask God if there is anything you're overlooking. And remember that not once does God convict us in order to make us feel like wretches. He's out to restore fellowship. Remember, God's pursuit is relationship. He initiates conversation through conviction, and we answer back through confession. Meanwhile, a miracle takes place. Heaven and earth, Immortal and mortal, Perfect and imperfect, engage in dialogue. Conviction is a hand-delivered invitation to meet with God, and confession is an RSVP with immediate arrival. Confession clears the path so the King of glory can come in. If you hold nothing back, neither will God.

Holy God, may I never get so prideful that I feel I can go for even a day without having sin to confess. Show me the attitudes, motives, and actions that displease You and block my relationship with You.

Who is a God like you, who pardons sin and forgives the transgression of the remnant of his inheritance? You do not stay angry forever but delight to show mercy.

Micah 7:18

The conversation God begins through conviction doesn't end with our response of confession. It continues with God telling us through His Word that He forgives us (1 John 1:9; Micah 7:18) and completes the process in our appropriate and freeing response of grateful acceptance. We will never stay out of that pit until we believe all the way to the marrow of our bones that God has forgiven us. Take a look at King Hezekiah's words to his God in Isaiah 38:17:

> In your love you kept me
> from the pit of destruction;
> you have put all my sins
> behind your back.

Here's how confession works: we lay all our sins at God's feet; He picks them up and throws all of them behind His back. In our Christian circles, we talk about putting our past behind us. That's not good enough. It's too easy for us to turn around and pick it up again. We want our past behind God's back. That way we'll have to go through God to get back to it. Admit that you can't beat a deal like that.

The religious police, however, warn us away from adopting the marrow-deep belief that we are forgiven. They're afraid God's complete removal of our debilitating load of guilt will make us feel so free that we'll throw caution to the winds and wander right back into that pit. Not so! The opposite is true. Few thinking people who feel squeaky clean for a change are compelled to dash right back into the mud. Almost always those folks who jump back into the pit never really believed what God says about them: *I have put all your sins behind My back.*

Oh Lord, I believe! Now help my unbelief so that, to the marrow of my bones, I can rest in the truth that You forgive my sins and put them behind Your back.

> *It is for freedom that*
> *Christ has set us free.*
>
> Galatians 5:1

ry out. Confess. And, the third step, *consent*. I love this one.

Consent is the most beautiful part of the process of getting out of a pit. There is no ambiguity about this step: it is definitely God's will. Determining God's will in so many other areas is less than certain. Like where He wants us to work. Where He wants us to move. Where He wants us to serve. Whom He wants us to date. Whether or not we should marry. This is not one of those uncertain areas: God wants you out of that pit. He wants you in victory. So all you have to do is *consent* to what He already wants for you.

Can you celebrate the simplicity of this step? Once you get the hang of it, I believe you will. First John 5:14–15 says, "This is the confidence we have in approaching God: that if we ask anything according to his will, he hears us. And if we know that he hears us—whatever we ask—we know that we have what we asked of him."

Beloved, God's will is for you to get out of that pit. If you will consent to the process and wait upon God as He begins shifting, shoving, and rearranging things for your release, you can go ahead and start getting excited, because it will happen. Just as God promises in His Word.

Look again at 1 John 5:14–15 and think about what it means to ask according to God's will—and what it means to you that He hears those requests.

Father, I believe it's Your will that I don't live in a pit. Help me cooperate with You. Help me consent to obeying Your will even as it takes me out of my familiar and comfortable surroundings.

Faith is confidence in what we hope for and assurance about what we do not see.

Hebrews 11:1

When I first introduced the three steps to you—cry out, confess, and consent—I told you that each of them involves your mouth. The ironic part of the process will be that you will most likely use your mouth before you use your faith. Here's why: for most of us who have failed over and over, our faith nearly disintegrated because somewhere along the way we confused faith in God with faith in ourselves. We've let ourselves down so many times that now we're nearly hopeless. In reality, however, we've given ourselves way too much credit. We think we're too much for God to handle. That the strength of our personal draw into the abyss exceeds the strength of God's draw to pull us out. Hence, we've rendered ourselves virtually faithless. The process can't just begin with our faith, because our faithlessness is our biggest problem. It's got to begin somewhere else.

Like with our mouths. So we're going to learn to speak out. And I don't mean mumbling under your breath. I want you to learn to cry out, confess, and consent using God's Word—and to do so, when at all possible, *out loud*. Volume is not the point. All you need is to have your own ears hear it. Why? I feel so strongly about this concept that I'm almost standing up at the keyboard to write it. Listen, beloved, "faith comes from hearing, and hearing by the word of Christ" (Romans 10:17 NASB).

What is one verse from Scripture that has been especially meaningful and significant in your walk of faith? Read it or say it out loud. Your faith will be built by hearing your own voice speak the words of Christ.

Lord, I'm excited about this experiment, about seeing how speaking out loud the words of Your Scripture will strengthen my faith in You, Your power, and Your love.

All Scripture is God-breathed and is useful for teaching, rebuking, correcting and training in righteousness.

2 Timothy 3:16

I have never come up with a more powerful way to pray than using Scripture. I will teach this method as long as I live, because I've seen such results from it. I don't always pray using Scripture, but when a serious situation arises, and particularly if it persists, I turn to God's Word every single time.

One reason Scripture is such a big help in prayer is because our challenges are often so overwhelming that we can't think of the right words to say. Another reason is because we can shift the burden of responsibility to God and His Word rather than ultimately crumbling under the weight of it ourselves. God's Word carries its own supernatural power. It's His very breath on the page that, when you voice it, you release into your own circumstances.

I can feel totally hopeless in a situation, but when

I begin to cry out, confess, and consent by speaking God's Word out loud, I soon feel the power of His Spirit start to fill me up from the tip of my toes to the top of my head. *Faith comes from hearing, and hearing by the Word of Christ.* My faith returns, and holy passion burns.

God loves His Word; therefore, if God's Spirit that lives inside a believer has not been quenched by unconfessed sin, God responds every time He hears it spoken.

On a related note, I'm so proud of you for getting this far into this devotional. I want so badly for you to be victorious, and I know you can be. God's Word tells me you can because you have the power of the entire Godhead behind you. You have the Father's will, the Son's Word, and the Holy Spirit's way. What more could you need?

Lord, this makes sense: that You can and will use Your Word to build up my faith in You and help me get out of my pit. Guide me to the verses you would have me pray as I cling to each word as a promise from You.

My word that goes out from my mouth:
It will not return to me empty,
but will accomplish what I desire
and achieve the purpose for which I sent it.

Isaiah 55:11

I'd like to give you a jump start so that you can get on with the process of letting God use your mouth to build up your faith. In tomorrow's devotional, you'll find some examples of Scriptures I've rewritten and incorporated into prayers for you. You'll see that the Scripture verses don't have to be used word for word. What's vital is that we echo the principles of Scripture so we can be certain that we're praying God's will.

I've offered Scripture Prayer samples to help you cry out, confess, and consent. At any point of the prayers, feel free to use your own words, pour out your heart, and get very specific with God. Use these starter prayers over and over for as many weeks as necessary until you're off and running on your own with at least some of the concepts in play. Don't let up when you begin to feel better. Feeling better is not what we're after. The goal is freedom from the pit *for the rest of your life.*

On days when you feel down, overwhelmed, or discouraged, get to your Scripture Prayers all the faster. On the days when you want to do it least, do it most. Be onto the enemy's devices. Show the enemy that if he messes with you, you'll just call out God's Word all the more. Nothing does him damage like the Sword of the Spirit.

Also expect your flesh to balk. It's been in control a long time, and it's not going to give over easily. No matter how resistant you feel, pray anyway. Whatever you do, don't quit.

Lord God, thank You that I don't stand alone or unarmed when the enemy strikes. Thank You for Your powerful Word. Please help me wield it with persistence and skill.

*You guide me with your counsel,
and afterward you will take me into glory.
Whom have I in heaven but you?
And earth has nothing I desire besides you.*

Psalm 73:24–25

So what does it look like to cry out, confess, and consent with Scripture Prayer? I'm very glad you asked. Here are the examples I promised.

Cry Out—I call to You, LORD, who are worthy of praise. From Your temple You hear my voice; my cry comes to Your ears (2 Samuel 22:4–7). O, my Strength, come quickly to help me. Rescue me from my powerful enemy and from foes who are too strong for me (Psalm 18:16–17). Bring me out into a spacious place; rescue me, LORD, because You delight in me (Psalm 18:19).

Confess—"Search me, God, and know my heart; test me and know my anxious thoughts. See if there is any offensive way in me, and lead me in the way everlasting" (Psalm 139:23–24). "I said, 'I will confess my transgressions to the LORD.' And you forgave the guilt of my sin" (Psalm 32:5). I confess that You are my Rock, my Fortress, and my Deliverer. You are my Rock, and I take refuge in You (2 Samuel 22:2).

Consent—If You are for me, who can be against me? You did not spare Your own Son but gave Him up for me. How will You not also graciously give me all things? (Romans 8:31–32). You know the plans You have for me, O God. Plans to prosper me and not to harm me. Plans to give me a hope and a future (Jeremiah 29:11). Thank You, God, for Your willingness to lead me to triumph (2 Corinthians 2:14).

Paul said, "Pray without ceasing" (1 Thessalonians 5:17 NASB), and I would add, "Pray God's Word as you do!"

Lord God, Your written Word is "living and active" (Hebrews 4:12). No wonder it makes sense to include Scripture verses in my prayers.

Praise the Lord, my soul;
all my inmost being, praise his holy name.
Praise the Lord, my soul,
and forget not all his benefits—
who forgives all your sins
and heals all your diseases,
who redeems your life from the pit
and crowns you with love and compassion,
who satisfies your desires with good things
so that your youth is renewed like the eagle's.

Psalm 103:1–5

God can deliver the most hardened criminal or the most hopeless addict in one second flat. With His eyes closed and His hands tied behind His back, if He has a mind to. I know people who made themselves at home in a pit a hundred feet deep and a thousand days long and, seemingly without warning, experienced the instantaneous deliverance of God. One moment they were in the throes of habitual sin—and the next moment they were free as birds.

Maybe God had marked His calendar for a little

instantaneous deliverance. I never doubt He can. I'm utterly elated when He does. Those are the kinds of testimonies that launch our faith to the moon and bring our congregations to their feet, cheering madly. I love it. I love to hear it. I love to see it.

But I have not one time experienced it. Let me say that again. Not one time. Not even an instantaneous deliverance for something comparatively shallow like a mini-pit of some kind I dug with a soupspoon instead of a shovel. I won't even be heel deep, and still I'll rarely walk away without a fight.

What experience with instantaneous deliverance have you had? Maybe, like me, you've seen it or heard about it. Maybe, unlike me, you've even experienced it.

Father, calling You "Lord" means trusting You to deliver me from my pit in Your perfect time and Your perfect way. Calling You "Lord" reminds me of Your great faithfulness in the past, in big ways and small. Calling You "Lord" gives me unspeakable peace and supernatural strength that can only come from You.

> *God . . . made his light shine in our hearts to give us the light of the knowledge of God's glory displayed in the face of Christ. But we have this treasure in jars of clay to show that this all-surpassing power is from God and not from us.*
>
> 2 Corinthians 4:6–7

I'm telling you, God and I work hard together. Maybe you consume a fair amount of divine energy yourself and, if so, perhaps we could sift some mutual encouragement out of the aggravation of never doing anything easily. I've come to the elementary conclusion that, to God, *together* is the whole point of any process.

Before He created human beings, God just said something and it happened. "Let there be light" and all. He could still do that. Sometimes He still does. But you might notice that a lot of that instantaneous action ceased after man came along—and obviously on God-purpose. Suddenly God wasn't so sudden. Time became the vehicle for this wonderful thing called history. You could neither rush it nor slow it. All you could do was ride it. What a ride it was for all those who preceded us.

And what a ride it is for us now. God etches history not on lands and nations but on human lives. Not on superhumans. Not even on particularly impressive humans, but on people prone to wandering and bruising, doubting and losing. God seems to summon the most faithless of all to faith. He is drawn to weakness, perhaps the ultimate proof that opposites really do attract.

Lord, You know even better than I do the ways I wander and doubt. You also know the bruises and losses I've experienced. And, although I wish I were more aware of Your presence with me in the moment, I thank You for never leaving me alone.

When you pass through the waters,
I will be with you;
and when you pass through the rivers,
they will not sweep over you.
When you walk through the fire,
you will not be burned;
the flames will not set you ablaze.
For I am the LORD, your God.

Isaiah 43:2–3

*T*hink about it. God could have accomplished in an instant many of the things that He decided to hammer out over the tedium of years. Sarai could have felt Isaac kick lustily within her before the dust of Ur was off Abram's sandals. God takes His own sweet time because sweet time is God's to take. Still, if man weren't around, I personally think He'd go back into the instant-action mode. Why wait if there's no one to wait with you? God created time for man. In fact, the words *in the beginning* mark the tick of the first clock. The Trinity has no such bounds in the eternal state. A wait is time oriented and, therefore, primarily man oriented. Perhaps among a host of other reasons, I think God often ordains a wait because He purely enjoys the togetherness of it.

Not long ago when I battled some health problems, a loving co-worker was a bit mystified over the distraction God had allowed in my life at a very busy time. I know I didn't need to take up for Him, but I did anyway. "I think He missed me," I told her. By the way she smiled, I knew she'd experienced exactly what I was talking about. In the relatively smooth days preceding the health issue, I had still sought God and served Him and, heaven knows, I still loved Him. But smooth living invariably, eventually, makes for sloppy spirituality. I want consuming fire to rage in my soul, and if it's got to come through fiery trial, so be it.

Think back over your life. What do you think God may have allowed you to experience because He missed you?

Lord, sloppy spirituality results from smooth living, and bittersweet fellowship can come when fiery trials do. Help me welcome those trials as an opportunity for fellowship with You.

Since ancient times no one has heard,
no ear has perceived,
no eye has seen any God besides you,
who acts on behalf of those who wait for him.

Isaiah 64:4

God is driven by relationship. His part in pit-deliverance is to lift you out. Your part is to hold on for dear life. Instantaneous deliverance motivates some people to cleave to Jesus. Others, after experiencing instantaneous deliverance, are thankful for a while, but soon we go our own way, assuring God that we'll call when we need Him again. Now that I think of it, the fact that I can't remember ever experiencing an instantaneous deliverance may not mean it hasn't happened. It may indicate it didn't end up meaning enough to me to remember it. But I digress . . .

Acting instantaneously or through a process, God does whatever works. If we approach God humbly for instantaneous deliverance, knowing good and well He can give it, yet He chooses instead to use the wagon of time, there is good news: we may have to wait for deliverance, but we never have to wait on God Himself. We never have to wait to enjoy His presence or be reassured of His love. If we're willing to take God at His Word, we can have any one of those relationship delights instantly. Also, huge things happen as you wait upon the Lord to deliver you from that pit. They begin the moment you cry out.

When you're convinced that you're no longer hopelessly stuck (you proved that when you cried out), when you resume a standing position against the enemy (you did that when you began confessing truth and consenting to God), and you're regaining glimpses of vision (you realize God doesn't hate you nor is He oblivious to you), you're no longer in the dark of the deep.

Deliverance and waiting for deliverance—thank You, Lord, for using both for my good and Your glory.

> *"I am the Alpha and the Omega," says the Lord God, "who is, and who was, and who is to come, the Almighty."*
>
> Revelation 1:8

Remember Psalm 40:1–2? The psalmist said that he "waited patiently for the LORD" who heard his cry and "lifted me out of the slimy pit." Don't get the idea that he sat around in the mire, sinking deeper every minute, telling God to take all the time He needed. The phrase *waited patiently* is translated from a single Hebrew word *qwh* (pronounced *kaw-VAW*).[1] In Isaiah 64:3, *qwh* is translated *expect*. The psalmist didn't sit in the pit and twiddle his muddy thumbs until God delivered him. He postured himself in absolute expectation. He had a goal, and his shoulders would not slump till he saw it fulfilled. His Deliverer was coming and, on His way, fighting bat-

1. Spiros Zodhiates, ed., "Lexical Aids to the Old Testament," *The Hebrew-Greek Key Word Study Bible*: #7747 (Chattanooga, TN: AMG Publishers, 1998), 1,548

tles and blazing paths somewhere beyond the psalmist's gaze.

Never fear that God is not at work while you wait. He's doing what no one else can. If your eyes could only see how God is moving all those chess pieces around the board for maximum impact, it would blow your mind. He's up to something big that doesn't affect only you. He's also after those around you. Furthermore, He's not just interested in impacting the present. He is the One "who is, and who was, and who is to come, the Almighty" (Revelation 1:8). Within every "is," God is mindful of what "was" and what "is to come," and He intends to show Himself mighty in all of the above. His agenda is not just to deliver you from the pit. His preeminent aim is to bring Himself fame, and you are one way He has chosen to do it. One thing is certain: you can't accuse God of being shortsighted.

I praise You, my faithful Deliverer, for Your involvement in my life in ways I can't even imagine.

I wait for the LORD, my whole being waits,
and in his word I put my hope.
I wait for the LORD
more than watchmen wait for the morning,
more than watchmen wait for the morning.

Psalm 130:5–6

*I*n Psalm 40, the Hebrew word *qwh* is translated "expect." In Psalm 130 (consider opening your Bible and reading the first six verses of Psalm 130), the word is also translated "wait," and the psalmist's eager expectation is beautifully clear from the context.

The psalmist watched for God like a civil watchman gazing at the horizon from atop the city wall, waiting for the victorious King to come into full view. According to the Lexical Aids of *The Complete Word Study Old Testament,* the Hebrew word *qwh* means "to lie in wait for someone . . . to expect, await, look for patiently, hope; to be confident, trust; to be enduring."[2]

---

2. Spiros Zodhiates and Warren Baker, eds., *The Complete Word Study Old Testament,* #6960 (Chattanooga, TN: AMG Publishers, 1994), 2360.

What does a watchman have to do with us? In God-terms, waiting means adopting a watchman's posture. His goal-orientation. After we've cried out to the one and only true Deliverer, we are exhorted by Scripture to exercise unwavering and daily confidence that God is coming to our rescue. That means ceasing to make ourselves comfortable in that pit another day. Spiritually speaking, stand up and watch. Anticipate your absolute, inevitable deliverance.

The psalmist puts his hope in God's promises, and we are blessed to have those written down for us. As you watch and anticipate, spend some time right now in God's Word and remind yourself of the promises God has made you. Don't know where to start? Psalm 23 is a good place.

My waiting for deliverance, Lord God, has not been a watchman's vigilant, this-is-my-job kind of waiting. Forgive me for my apathy—and may Your Word fuel my trust in Your faithfulness, Your goodness, and Your perfect timing.

> Can a mother forget the baby at her
> breast and have no compassion on the
> child she has borne? Though she may
> forget, I will not forget you! See, I have
> engraved you on the palms of my hands.
>
> God's message to Israel in Isaiah 49:15–16

*T*here is another definition of the Hebrew word *qwh* besides watching and anticipating which is my favorite: *The Complete Word Study Old Testament* tells us it also means "to bind together (by twisting)."[3] Let me help you picture what this means.

After I had experienced a lifetime full of dysfunctional relationships and inevitably unmet expectations, motherhood somehow turned out to be everything I imagined it to be. More than I imagined it to be. Nothing had ever hit me with that kind of gale force. I'd been had by something my husband said wasn't even the size of an impressive striped bass but had about the same

---

3. Spiros Zodhiates and Warren Baker, eds., *The Complete Word Study Old Testament*, #6960 (Chattanooga, TN: AMG Publishers, 1994), 2360.

amount of hair. With her almost indiscernible infant breath, Amanda huffed and puffed and blew down the house I'd built around my heart.

Having foreseen and perfectly timed the opportunity, God wisely used my firstborn to make my getting well and becoming a whole person finally worth any amount of work it required. Sadly, I didn't like myself enough to do it just for me. Sadder still, I didn't trust God enough at that time to do it for Him.

When God gave me Amanda, He knew that I finally held something in my arms so precious and yet so emotionally vulnerable I'd do anything not to totally mess her up. Who or what has motivated you—or at least *helped* motivate you—to get well and to work on climbing out of a pit and becoming a whole person?

Almighty God, You who, through Jesus' death on the cross, saved me from the pit of eternal death can save me from the pit I've called home for too long. Thank You for Your powerful and persistent love.

Twenty-two years old and the first in my group of friends to be a mom, I didn't have a clue what to do with a toddler, so I did what came naturally. I played with her. We had a repertoire of games, but one was Amanda's favorite. It always came at the end of play time when I told her that Mommy needed to straighten up the house before Daddy got home. I'd take on a certain dead-giveaway tone and tell her she could go right on playing while I got to work. That was code for "climb on." She'd grin and act like she was going about her business, but when I turned my head, she'd throw her arms around my thigh and put both little feet on one of mine.

I knew the game well, so I'd start putting dishes in the sink and clothes in the washer, pretending I was oblivious to the tiny tot I was dragging along on my leg. I'd call, "Amanda? Where'd you go? I can't find you anywhere! Answer your mother this second!" She'd giggle her head off.

Dragging her from room to room, I'd look behind the furniture and in the closet, all the while calling her name. When she couldn't bear it any more, she'd yell, "I'm right here, silly Mommy! Look right down here!" I'd glance down with pretend shock and squeal like she'd scared me half to death. We'd laugh ourselves silly . . . then we'd do it again the next day.

Amanda and I loved to pick up before Keith got home—it was good for our hearts and built an intimacy between us. What routine builds intimacy between you and your heavenly Father?

You love me with a Father's love. Lord, please redeem that metaphor for me and teach me to receive Your love, the love of my perfect Parent.

> *Those who hope in the L*ORD
> *will renew their strength.*
> *They will soar on wings like eagles;*
> *they will run and not grow weary,*
> *they will walk and not be faint.*

Isaiah 40:31

Amanda taught Melissa her favorite game the moment Little Sister was barely old enough to stand up and hang on. I'd walk all over the house with those two munchkins atop my aching feet. By the time I was supposed to call out their names, I was out of breath.

So why all the details about fun at the Moore home? Because Amanda and Melissa offer a picture of what I want you to understand, a picture of *qwh*.

While you wait for God to work and to manifest your sure deliverance, wrap yourself around Him as tightly as you possibly can. Ask Him to make you more God-aware than you have ever been in your life. Bind yourself to Him with everything you've got so that you will ultimately—inevitably—go anywhere He does. Hang on for dear life and never let go. No matter how long it takes, He'll never run out of breath or stop to soak His aching feet. Pin yourself so close to Him that you can hear Him whisper. His words will live in you and you will live in Him.

What keeps you from putting your feet onto God's? What keeps you from clinging to His leg and hanging on for dear life? God does not make His home in a pit. Bound to His holy robe, neither will you.

As I hope in You, Lord, may I find the strength You promise, strength to hang on to You, to bind myself to Your holy robe, so I will no longer make a pit my home.

Shout for joy, you heavens;
rejoice, you earth;
burst into song, you mountains!
For the LORD comforts his people
and will have compassion on his afflicted ones.

Isaiah 49:13

So how do you know when you're finally out of that pit? Two ways. Psalm 40:2 describes the first one:

> He lifted me out of the slimy pit,
> out of the mud and mire;
> he set my feet on a rock
> and gave me a firm place to stand.

One way you know you're out is when you realize after all the slip-sliding and sky diving you've done, your feet are finally planted on a rock, and you've got a firm place to stand. It means you've found a steady place where you can stand up and rest your whole weight on your feet without fear of eventually discovering you're knee-deep in new quicksand. Even if the mountains fall into the sea, you're secure. Even if the seas overtake the shores, you're not going anywhere. If earthly rulers fall and stock markets crash, your feet are steadfast. Knees needn't wobble. As long as you rest all your weight on that rock, you're not going to fall. Winds may blow and waters rise, but you will not lose ground. Praise His steadfast name, God is not a divine rug someone can pull out from under your feet.

Airlines have weight limits on luggage, and there's been talk about passengers paying for a ticket according to their own poundage as well. Thankfully, God has no limitations or extra fees. God can hold your weight—the full emotional, spiritual, mental, and physical poundage of you—sixty seconds a minute, sixty minutes an hour, twenty-four hours a day, seven days a week, 365 days a year for the rest of your life.

You are solid ground for my life; You offer security and safety. Great are You, my Deliverer, my God!

God is not a divine rug someone can pull out from under your feet. Nor is He a fad.

I remember when one of my neighbors realized I was in "religious" work after we'd enjoyed a very natural and amiable cul-de-sac relationship for several years. She already knew we were Christians, but somehow learning what I did for a living put her over the edge. Trust me, I didn't tell. Someone squealed on me. My heart sank when she suddenly felt uncomfortable around me and needlessly scrambled for some kind of common ground for conversations. The conversations about our kids had worked well before, but her newfound knowledge of my work tricked her into thinking they were too trivial to talk about anymore. I could see her going through her mental Rolodex turning like a hamster on a wheel. As if a cartoon light bulb popped over her head, she all at once recalled a close relative and blurted out, "He had a religious spell, too, when he had that skin cancer."

God is unreasonably patient and merciful. He's there for every urgent need and any sudden spell, but an emergency room relationship with God is not the psalmist's idea of a firm place to stand. God is not a drive-thru drugstore. He is not just a temporary fix in an urgent situation or a good side to get on when we need Him to save our scrawny necks. God wants to be part of your life all day every day, now and always.

It's easy to turn to You when the going gets rough. Please keep me mindful of You—of my need for You and of Your faithfulness to me—when the road is smooth.

*I consider everything a loss because of the
surpassing worth of knowing Christ Jesus
my Lord, for whose sake I have lost all things.
I consider them garbage, that I may gain
Christ and be found in him, not having a
righteousness of my own that comes from the
law, but that which is through faith in Christ.*

Philippians 3:8–9

God is not just a firm place to stand. He's a firm place to stay. This book is not about getting out of the pit for a while. It's about getting out of the pit for good. And if that's what we want, we've got to do something absolutely crucial: we've got to make up our minds. The ground beneath our feet will be only as firm as our resolve. God *gives* us a firm place to stand, but we have to decide we want to take it. John 3:16 tells us that "God so loved the world that he gave his one and only Son," but He doesn't force anyone to take Him. Each individual gets to exercise the prerogative as to whether or not to be a taker. God is the consummate Giver, extending salvation, hope, and significance. Be a taker!

Thank You for calling me to know the truth about Jesus. May I come to value it—and salvation through Him and my relationship with You—even more than I do already.

They would put their trust in God
and would not forget his deeds
but would keep his commands.
They would not be like their ancestors—
a stubborn and rebellious generation,
whose hearts were not loyal to God,
whose spirits were not faithful to him.

Psalm 78:7–8

God gives us a firm place to stand, but we have to decide we want to take it. And we take the firm place He gives when we make up our minds and plant both our feet. That's exactly what the Hebrew word translated *firm* in Psalm 40:2 means. In another psalm it is used to characterize man's response to God. Read above how the psalmist Asaph describes a generation of takers that chooses to receive God's love and respond with trust, obedience, and loyalty.

And that word *loyal* comes from the very same Hebrew word as *firm*. God's complaint about the Israelites in Psalm 78 was their inability to make up their minds about

Him. Were they with Him or not? Did they want a firm place to stand or an emergency room to visit? Like us, they wanted God when they were in trouble, but as soon as the pressure let up, they wanted to chart their own course and be their own boss. The momentary revelry of their rebellion turned into terrible bouts of captivity and consequences. They experienced what we do: the slide into the pit is the only thrill ride. From that point on, a pit's just dirt.

Did you see anything about yourself in the mirror that the previous paragraph holds up to you? Maybe you thought about your emergency room visits, your desire to chart your own course, or your own thrill ride into a pit.

Yes, a pit's just dirt. It's crazy that we often choose it.

Lord, may my life be characterized by trust in You, remembrance of Your goodness to me, obedience to Your commands, loyalty to You, and faithfulness to Your lordship of my life.

163

> *If we died with him, we will also live with him; if we endure, we will also reign with him. If we disown him, he will also disown us; if we are faithless, he will remain faithful, for he cannot disown himself.*

2 Timothy 2:11–13

So will you and I be takers of what God gives? And if or when we say yes, will you and I be loyal to Him?

At its very core, loyalty means a made-up mind. It means that certain questions are already answered before life asks them. Since it shares the same definition as firm, *loyal* in Psalm 78 means to be "sure . . . certain . . . ready . . . prepared . . . determined." It means we've settled some things in advance of the inevitable temptation to revert or destructively scratch a temporary itch. It means we don't wait until the heat of the moment to decide. You know what I'm talking about. A loyal spouse doesn't wait until someone flirts with her at work to decide if she's going to be faithful. She has already made the decision to stand by her man before a circumstance posed the question.

That's how God is about you. He's firm. He's loyal. He made up his mind about you before the foundation of the world. Regardless of who has betrayed you and what promises they didn't keep, God is firm in His commitment to you.

Will you be loyal and firm in your commitment to Him? Read the words of 2 Timothy 2. Those are words from a loyal follower, words about the blessings that come with loyalty and consequences of disloyalty.

God is firm in His commitment to you. Savor that truth.

Only by Your grace, Lord God, will I be able to remain loyal to You and firm in my commitment to You. Thank You that You abound in grace, because a never-ending supply is definitely what I need.

Because of the LORD's great love we
are not consumed, for his compassions
never fail. They are new every morning;
great is your faithfulness.

Lamentations 3:22–23

*G*od is firm in His decision to love you as His child. God is loyal in His commitment to you. He will never change His mind about your value. Circumstances won't cause Him to rethink His position. Even if you, like me, have made multiple trips to the pit, His affection for you is unwavering. He's all yours if you want Him. The Rock is yours for the standing. Without hesitation God offers you a firm place to stand, but your feet are not firmly set in place until you've made up your own mind that's where you want to be. He will not force you to stand. And He most assuredly will not force you to stay.

I'll tell you why I'm hammering the point. Until you finally make up your mind that you're cleaving to

God and calling upon His power from now until Hades freezes over, your feet are set upon a banana peel. You may stand while the wind is calm, but when the storm hits and the floodwaters rise, the undertow will leave you gulping for air.

God is firm, unbending, immovable in His eternal commitment to you.

Lord, as I consider your firm, unbending, immovable commitment to me, I am humbled by my shaky, wavering, transitory commitment to You. Forgive me, Lord—and thank You for Your faithfulness to me despite my faithlessness.

Our struggle is not against flesh and blood,
but against the rulers, against the authorities,
against the powers of this dark world and
against the spiritual forces of evil in the
heavenly realms. . . . [So] take up the shield
of faith, with which you can extinguish
all the flaming arrows of the evil one.

Ephesians 6:12, 16

*A*re you standing on a banana peel? That's okay until a storm hits. Then you'll find yourself gulping for air. Case in point . . .

My friend with a fierce drug dependency problem spoke to me recently of her extreme frustration with relapses and her confusion concerning her intermittent bouts of victory. She explained that she does "so well in between" crises. She gets along great as long as her ex-husband doesn't do something to remind her of rejection. She stays consistent as long as her kids don't have problems in school. She pedals along beautifully if she can pay her bills. She thinks that if she could rid herself of the problems that tempt her to drug use, she could stay on her feet.

The problem is, life on Planet Earth consists of one crisis after another. Beloved, this I promise you. Circumstances will offer unceasing invitations back to the pit. If our souls had no enemy, life on clay feet would still be hard. But the fact is we do have an enemy, and he formulates one scheme after another. He knows how to trip your switch. He finds your Achilles' heel, and that's where he aims his darts. And if he's anything at all, he's a great shot.

In what ways have you been especially aware of his marksmanship skills?

Lord, You tell us that we'll have trials in this world, and You aren't kidding! You also tell us that You have overcome the world with all its tribulations (John 16:33). Come quickly, Lord!

> *No temptation has overtaken you except what is common to mankind. And God is faithful; he will not let you be tempted beyond what you can bear. But when you are tempted, he will also provide a way out so that you can endure it.*
>
> 1 Corinthians 10: 13

*I*t's always a good strategy to know one's enemy. We've seen, for instance, that Satan is quite a wise, scheming, and skilled marksman. The Deceiver is also very persistent in his efforts to discourage, if not dissuade, God's people. He also attacks God's people as the Tempter.

You can insulate yourself from temptation for only so long. At some point you have to get out there, plant your own two feet upon that rock, and resist. Once, then twice. Ten times, then twenty-five. Thirty times, then fifty, till your flesh submits and your enemy gives up on that front and quits. Sooner or later, relying on the power of Christ acting through you, you're going to have to face your foe and win. You can't just run from him and hide, because he'll keep showing up wherever you go.

Details from my life remind me of that fact regularly. I've encountered bears in Wyoming and gators in Florida. And there are hurricanes in Houston. Tornadoes in Kansas. Earthquakes in California. Avalanches in Everest. Tsunamis in Asia. Welcome to life on our planet. Wherever you go, there's a foe.

But our God is omnipotent, omniscient. Omnipresent. . . . All-powerful. All-knowing. Always everywhere. . . . Sounds like exactly the kind of God we need on a planet where our foe is wherever we go!

Lord, the enemy will keep showing up, but I know You will always be with me. Keep me mindful of that truth in the moment, whatever foe or temptation I'm facing.

*L*ife on Planet Earth consists of one crisis after another. And circumstances on this planet will offer unceasing invitations back to the pit. The same gravity that sticks our feet to the floor throws curve balls through our air. One day we're well. The next day we're sick. At Christmas we get a bonus. In January we're in debt. If your victory depends on the right circumstances, you may as well wave the white flag and surrender to defeat. Just go ahead and take that snort. Gulp that fourth gin and tonic. Binge and purge that pizza, a side of garlic bread, and a half gallon of mint chocolate chip. Sleep with that jerk again. Eat, drink, and be miserable.

Or you could make up your mind that you're in with God, standing upon that rock, for the rest of your days. The apostle Paul called it being found in Christ (Philippians 3:9). No matter how long it's been since you've seen me, He is where you can find me. I've made up my mind.

Choosing to be in with God, to stand upon that rock, is a decision we'll make for the rest of our days. Usually several times a day.

You, Lord God, are all sufficient. You are my Provider and Guide, my Protector and Defender, my Fortress and, yes, my Rock. Teach me to live in You, whatever life holds.

Your kingdom is an everlasting kingdom,
and your dominion endures
through all generations.
The LORD is trustworthy in all he promises
and faithful in all he does.
The LORD upholds all who fall
and lifts up all who are bowed down.

Psalm 145:13–14

Whether my health flourishes or fails, I'll be in Christ. Richer or poorer, in the light of day or dark of night, find me in Christ. Spouse or not. Kids or not. Job or not. I've made up my mind.

When you've made that decision and given your heart, mind, and soul in all their fissured parts; and when you've given your past, present, and future "to him who is able to keep you from falling" (Jude 1:24); and when you know you're absolutely in, come what may . . . congratulations, sweet thing. You're out of the pit and your feet are on a rock.

Having a firm place to stand doesn't mean life isn't hard and temptations don't come. It doesn't mean you get everything right. It doesn't mean you don't sin, although you won't be able to wallow in it like you used to. It just means you've determined your position no matter what comes your way.

Life gives opportunity after opportunity to choose to stand on the Rock of the Lord. And when it does, you may sway back and forth. You may curl up in a ball or buck like a bronco. But you've decided where you're putting your feet—on the Rock. And once you're there, it's a mighty firm place to stand.

Help me live out the vow implied in calling You "Lord": "Whether my health flourishes or fails, I'll be in Christ. Richer or poorer. In the light of day or dark of night. Spouse or not. Kids or not. Job or not. I've made up my mind. Find me in Christ."

> *The Sovereign LORD is my strength; he makes my feet like the feet of a deer, he enables me to tread on the heights.*
>
> Habakkuk 3:19

*I*n case you're wondering, you and I can live in the pit and still be Christians, but we will live a tragic portion of our lives in ever-deepening misery and insecurity. Our feet will become like drill bits, spiraling us deeper and deeper until we sink so low into despair that we forget the scent of fresh air and the feeling of sunshine. If we've genuinely received Christ as our personal Savior, our salvation is secure. Eternal security is not the question. Earthly security is. Treating God like the divine drive-thru pharmacy where we can get a quick fix, we will live in a constant state of insecurity and uncertainty. Tums by day, Sominex by night.

With all due respect—and from one who has been there—it's time to make up your mind. Not only for all the reasons we've just discussed, but also for one other. You'd better brace yourself, because it's a whopper. Here's the pitiful truth, as well as I know how to tell it: there's nothing quite like trying to stay out of the pit while others close to you are still in it. I don't think I have to tell you that a whole family can take up residency in a deluxe-sized pit with personalized compartments. So can a whole set of friends. Yep, right there on 105 South Pit Drive. Looks like a house. Acts like a pit. Make no mistake. A pit is an excellent place for a pileup.

The biggest challenge you may face is trying to stay out of the pit while those close to you are still in it, but I think you're up for it.

Lord, may I find in You the strength I need, however strong the pull back to the pit is.

> *"What is impossible with man*
> *is possible with God."*
>
> Jesus in Luke 18:27

*P*ileups happen. Especially in families. That's what happened to mine. That's what happened to Keith's. That's the nature of family. The ties are so close that the same cord that hangs one tangles all. They say alcoholism is a family disease, but it's not the only one. Both of my girls experienced some secondhand effects from my childhood victimization—Amanda battled outright fears, Melissa battled inward trust. And heaven knows my husband was affected just as I was by his family's losses.

Families pile up, but no matter who is at the bottom of it, no one is a lost cause. No one is too heavy to be pulled out. God delivers with "a mighty hand and an outstretched arm" (Deuteronomy 5:15). But He does it one person at a time. Remember, what He's after is relationship. What He wants takes place one-on-one. Nobody gets delivered on somebody else's coattail. Nobody gets out hanging onto somebody else's ankle. Jesus pulls each willing party out of the pit, one person at a time. And with His own scarred hand, by the way, just in case you think He doesn't get our pain.

What cord in the generations of your family seems to have tangled you and/or your children? Remember, no one is beyond Jesus' saving reach! No pileup is beyond His careful and merciful untangling! And He who suffered and died on the cross definitely understands your pain.

Lord, God, thank You for today's encouragement, for this truth rooted in Your unchanging nature and steadfast character. Life would be even more difficult if I couldn't hope in You!

"No one who has left home or brothers or sisters or mother or father or children or fields for me and the gospel will fail to receive a hundred times as much in this present age . . . and in the age to come eternal life."

Jesus in Mark 10:29–30

*I*f you're the first one who escapes a family pileup, you'd think your fellow pit-dwellers would be happy that at least you got out. You'd think your deliverance would give them hopes of their own, but for some reason that's often not the way it works. Usually when you get out of the pit, somebody in the family feels betrayed that you felt a change was necessary. They think it means you're saying something is wrong with the rest of them. Sometimes when a person decides to have a mind made up toward God and feet firmly set upon a rock, loyalty to Him is misinterpreted as disloyalty toward family.

Actually, nothing has the potential for greater

positive impact in a close-knit group of people than when one decides to break tradition and pursue another level of wholeness. But I am convinced that health can be even more contagious than infirmity. Until the breakthrough comes, however, and the Jesus-virus catches, you better glue your feet to that rock. The pressure to resume your old rank can be titanic. Family pressure to maintain your current status or to resume your old rank once you've escaped the pit will be great—but the strength God provides is greater!

Lord, I trust You to help me stand strong against the attempts I'll face at swaying me back into my pit. And please make the health I'm pursuing contagious to the family members who are affected.

Teach me to do your will,
for you are my God;
may your good Spirit
lead me on level ground.

Psalm 143:10

When my beloved mother went home to be with the Lord, she was out of sorts with me. Had been for several years. That conflict was not outright, but it was so strong that the undercurrent nearly swept me under. It was cold war. The Antarctic kind. I tried to talk to her about it, but she wouldn't admit that we had something between us. The rupture began when I wrote *Breaking Free*. The book was too serious for her.

I begged her to understand. Appealed to her sense of compassion. "Mom, people are hurting so badly. They don't need another motivational speech. They need freedom from countless abuses and addictions. They've been through all sorts of sufferings. They need to see the power of God's Word at work in a real, fallible person. They need people like us to fess up to our pain."

Nope, she thought they just needed to get on with

it like she did after some bad stuff happened to her in childhood.

I love my family of origin. I never wanted to do anything but honor them. I never wrote an ill word about them, but my mom felt strongly that my admission to having been abused by a person close to the family and turning out decidedly dysfunctional reflected negatively upon the entire family.

Lest you misunderstand, not for one second did I lose my mother's love. I always knew that she loved me. She just tried to quit showing it so much, and she quit saying it entirely.

In what ways, if any, has God used my brutal honesty to help you?

The truth does set us free, Lord, but the process can involve pain and the loss of relationships, perhaps temporary, perhaps permanent. Please walk me through this process on this path of freedom from the pit.

> *All these people were still living by faith*
> *when they died. They did not receive*
> *the things promised; they only saw them*
> *and welcomed them from a distance.*
>
> Hebrews 11:13

Despite the cheesy picture decking the front of the Christmas card (yes, we send out those cards too), no family is perfect, and perhaps none less so than the one that tries to convince us it is. At the Moore home, we've given that up. We're not cynical, though, because we know as well as anyone that entire families can be changed. I've seen it for myself. I am currently watching it happen in my own family of origin, but what has already happened in Keith's is nothing less than stunning. He and I have asked God to chase down every member of our extended families and make them His own. To heal any brokenness with His love and make every life matter. We've asked Him for such a mark on our family line that no generation will be without lovers of His Word, teachers of His truth, and followers of His way—right up to the very return of Christ.

If I were a wagering woman, I'd have placed my money on this happening in my family first, but the chase God has placed on Keith's has been relentless. We never really expected to see with our own human eyes much of the change we requested from God in our family lines. We expected to die seeing it in the distance and believing it all the same.

When has God surprised you by allowing you to see an answer to a prayer that you, in your heart of hearts, truly didn't expect to see?

I know, Lord God, that You do not want anyone to perish! I thank You for those opportunities to celebrate with You when someone I love enters Your family for eternity.

Love is patient, love is kind. . . . it is not
proud. It does not dishonor others, it is
not self-seeking, it is not easily angered, it
keeps no record of wrongs. Love does not
delight in evil but rejoices with the truth.

1 Corinthians 13:4–6

So was it worth it? Was getting out of the pit worth the results? Was it worth not just accepting the family status quo but believing God for a better way? A healthier way? Was it worth being misunderstood? Was it worth being told you think you're better than them? Is it really possible to still treasure what you love most about your family's ways but exercise the prerogative to dump what you don't? You bet it is. Little by little Keith and I watched family resentment turn into at least a hint of respect and, at most, a holy jealousy to have for themselves what we had found.

Sometimes the biggest favor you could ever do for your loved ones is the hardest. Nobody gets the right to keep you in a pit or to shame you for bailing.

When God performs a dramatic deliverance in our lives, the nature of some of our closest relationships inevitably changes. The healthier we get, the more we realize how unhealthy we were. We find out where we've been motivated by guilt more than God. Or, for crying out loud, more than *love*.

Lord, pure love does not delight in shame, guilt, or a painful status quo. Help me to recognize the difference between the old lies I've believed for so long and your true, healing love.

We were therefore buried with him through baptism into death in order that, just as Christ was raised from the dead through the glory of the Father, we too may live a new life.

Romans 6:4

Cooperating with God through painful relationship transitions may be the hardest work of all in our deliverance from the pit. Persevere with Him and trust Him—not just with your life, but also with their lives. You weren't doing them any favors by staying in the pit with them, despite what they say. Keep your feet upon that Rock no matter how plaintively beloved voices call from the pit and beg you to come quickly. Just as you waited upon God for your own deliverance, wait upon Him for theirs. Pray hard for them. Love them lavishly, but as a Rock-dweller, not a fellow pit-dweller.

As you accomplish such an impressive feat, don't let the enemy tempt you into developing a prideful spirit because you're out and they're still in. Pride is the fastest track back. Through Christ alone "we have gained access by faith into this grace in which we now stand" (Romans 5:2). Your commitment to them from this new position has never been more vital.

Then again, not everybody is family; not every tie of the heartstring is God's will, and not every relationship needs to change. Some of them need to end. Just flat end. I don't know a nice way to say this. Some relationships won't survive your deliverance from the pit. And most of those don't need to.

Just as you trust God with your life, you can trust Him with those people you may need to separate from. In fact, you may be able to do absolutely nothing more than that for them.

What relationship, if any, came to mind when you read "Not every relationship needs to change. Some of them need to end"? What was your initial reaction? What is your prayer?

Lord God, the path to newness of life isn't easy. I'm glad You're walking it with me.

The LORD is my rock, my fortress
and my deliverer.

2 Samuel 22:2

Maybe that was a tough note to end on, thinking about the fact that some relationships won't survive your deliverance from the pit—and that most of those don't need to. One reason is, you discover that the pit was all you had in common and that, under different circumstances, you wouldn't even have been drawn together. We can hope that this person is not your spouse. If it is, however, start seeking God for a miracle just as Keith and I did. But if it's not a relationship God blesses and not one His Word binds you to, it needs candid examination.

Start with the one you're most afraid of losing. You think you can't live without that person, but that's not true. Infused with Christ's all-surpassing power, you are so much tougher than you think you are. So I'm going to say it to you like I felt God say it to me: quit acting like a wimp. And quit the whining. It's depleting energy you need for the great escape. God has somewhere astounding to take you, and if you've got some people who won't let you go, you need to let them go.

You may ask, "Aren't we supposed to keep loving people no matter how messed up they are?" Absolutely, and sometimes letting go of them is the most loving thing we can do. If the person was unhealthy for you, it's highly likely that you were equally unhealthy for him or her. In no way do I mean to minimize the difficulty of walking away from some destructive relationships, but if all we do is focus on the hardship, we'll never get out of the mud. Our disfigured sympathies will keep us knee-deep in the mire, and our love will turn into resentment.

Lord, teach me to love wisely and to live boldly by Your grace and in Your power.

Be strong and courageous. Do not be afraid or terrified . . .for the LORD your God goes with you; he will never leave you nor forsake you.

Deuteronomy 31:6

*A*sk yourself something I've had to ask myself in my pursuit of freedom: Which of your relationships are fueled by genuine affection, and which are fueled by addiction? I don't know about you, but I've done exactly what the apostle Paul accused the Galatians of doing. I've started relationships in the Spirit that somewhere along the way veered into the flesh (Galatians 3:3). Regardless of how we began, we can become as emotionally addicted to a relationship as to a substance.

Beware of anyone who tries to become indispensable to you. Who becomes the one to whom you repeatedly say, "You're the only person on earth I can possibly trust." If that's really true, then you're not getting out enough. In fact, I'd be willing to bet that he or she is the biggest reason you're not getting out. Boldly identify any "pusher" in your life, anyone who keeps feeding the unhealthy part of you because it feeds the unhealthy part of her. Or of him. Question an inability to be alone. Is it possible that God can't even get to you because of that person? As we near the end of this journey together, I beg you to let no one "love" you to death.

It takes courage to remove one's self from unhealthy relationships. But God will provide that courage.

Lord, You call me to a life of balance. Please guide me as I navigate relational waters, that I may be investing in healthy relationships and moving away from unhealthy ones.

*B*e brave, beloved. Be brave! Do the hard thing. Let that person go if that's what God is telling you. Remember what Keith said to me? Good-bye is a necessary life skill. Exercise it with a confidence only God can give you and don't beat around the bush when you do it. Has He not commanded you? "Be strong and courageous. Do not be terrified; do not be discouraged, for the LORD Your God will be with you wherever you go" (Joshua 1:9).

Say good-bye to that pit once and for all. Living up in the fresh air and sunshine where your feet are upon the Rock and your head is above your enemy's is not for the fainthearted. It's for those who make up their minds.

When has saying good-bye proved to be a wise and healthy move for you? Think about the good that God has blessed you with since that good-bye.

While we're talking about relationships, I've found that my connection to the Lord helps my relationships with others. You might want to see if the One impacts the others.

Lord, transform my heart that I might be more sensitive to Your guiding presence in my life and more able to love others with a pure, healthy love.

They sang a new song, saying: "You are worthy to take the scroll and to open its seals, because you were slain, and with your blood you purchased for God persons from every tribe and language and people and nation."

Revelation 5:9

*Y*ou will have a new song in your mouth, a hymn of praise to your God. That's the second way you'll know you've waved good-bye to the pit. Right after the psalmist tells us that God sets us on the rock and gives us a firm place to stand, he tells us God gives us a new song: "He put a new song in my mouth, a hymn of praise to our God" (Psalm 40:3).

Every one of us was born for song. Even the one who hasn't turned on his radio since the invention of the cell phone. Even the one who wouldn't mind church so much if it weren't for the singing. The one who came for a sermon, not all that getting up and down. The one who wonders why some people don't feel silly about how they act during the music at church. The one who just doesn't get it—and doesn't think she wants to.

It doesn't matter whether you have a beautiful voice or make mostly noise, you were born for song. And not just any kind of song. Your heart beats to the rhythm of a God-song, and your vocal cords were fashioned to give it volume.

Music is a gift from God to man. Your singing of a new song is a gift to Him.

Forgive me for any reluctance I have about singing my heartfelt praise to You. Free me so I may whole-heartedly celebrate You!

*A*s amazing, awe inspiring, and soul-elevating as a symphony can be, a God-song in the simplest man's soul is more than that. It's not just a moment. It's not just an emotional intoxication. It's the unleashed anthem of a freed soul. A song expresses something no amount of spoken words can articulate, no amount of nonverbal affection can demonstrate. Music is its own thing, especially when instruments and voices respond to the tap of the divine Conductor. Nothing can take a song's place. If its outlet gets clogged, the soul gets heavier and heavier.

And nothing on earth clogs the windpipe like the polluted air of a pit.

But that doesn't seem to be the case for everyone. Think about how often you've tried to affirm someone for his strength in a certain tribulation, and he wouldn't take the compliment. He knows the fear he faces in the night, just like we do. He is painfully well acquainted with his own weakness when no one's looking, just like we are. I don't believe many people think themselves strong. We can hear countless sermons on joy through tribulation, but we're not sure we've ever had the spiritual fortitude to do anything but whine through ours. And whining is not the same as singing.

Lord, I praise You for the way song points me to You and lightens my heart. May I choose singing over whining!

Sing to the LORD a new song,
for he has done marvelous things. . . .
Shout for joy to the LORD, all the earth,
burst into jubilant song with music.

Psalm 98:1, 4

Beloved, a song of praise freely sung and spontaneously offered is one of the most blatant trademarks of joy in tribulation. You have not let that situation get to you entirely and bury you in a pit until you've lost your God-song. Likewise, you know you're out of that pit when you not only have your old songs returned but something fresh has happened. God has put a new song in your mouth. A brand-new hymn of praise to your God.

Having a new song in our mouths doesn't mean we're completely out of the pain that caused our pit or the pain that our pit caused. It doesn't even mean, if ours was a pit of sin, that all the consequences are necessarily behind us. It just means we're no longer stuck. No longer defeated. No longer caked in mud. Our vision is returning. Hints of creativity are reemerging. It's a new day, God doesn't hate us after all, and we can't help but praise Him.

I remember vividly every detail in my ascent from the worst pit of my life. I was driving home by myself from church on a winter night ablaze with brilliant stars, still in acute emotional pain from the situation I'd been in. Singing at the top of my lungs with the praise music blaring from my car speakers, I slid back my sunroof and screamed over and over, "I am free!"

As I sang aloud in my car in that glorious winter night, I was a long way from being out of pain but make no mistake, I was out of that pit, and I absolutely knew I was not going back.

Going back into a pit is a choice, Lord. Please enable me to choose to stay out of the pit for good.

*H*aving a new song in our mouths doesn't necessarily mean we've learned three verses to a brand-new hymn replete with a chorus we've never heard before. It could happen that way. You could come out of a season of difficulty where a new Christian contemporary song or a praise and worship chorus becomes the expression of a fresh wave of love and awareness of Christ. Sometimes during worship at my church, when the band begins a song that holds significance to me, I want to glance up toward heaven and say to Jesus, "They're playing our song."

When that happens, it's a wonderful moment, but

it's not what the psalmist means when he calls us to sing a new song. He means that a whole new level of praise erupts from a delivered soul. It's as if a lid pops off of an undiscovered canyon somewhere deep inside, and a dam of living water breaks, rinses, and fills it. A testimony of God's goodness springs from the well to the lips. Music comes alive and suddenly puts words to what you feel. You have a song on your heart that can't help but find its way—in various words and melodies—to your mouth. To some degree, we're all psalmists. We all need song.

There's nothing quite like being able to say to the God of the universe, "They're playing our song."

Lord, thank you for the indescribable joy I feel when a song about You resonates through my soul. I pray that my new thoughts, new actions, and new relationships will be a sweet melody to You.

> *"Where were you when I laid the earth's
> foundation? Tell me, if you understand. Who
> marked off its dimensions? Surely you know!
> Who stretched a measuring line across it?
> On what were its footings set, or who laid its
> cornerstone—while the morning stars sang
> together and all the angels shouted for joy?"*
>
> God in Job 38:4–7

Music is as eternal as the Holy Trinity, ever attempting to fill God's boundless space with infinite echoes of majesty. The Father, Son, and Holy Spirit were surely the originators and trio emeritus of three-part harmony. According to Holy Writ, they apparently considered that something as marvelous and miraculous as the creation of Planet Earth needed accompaniment. Since each member of the Trinity would be busy doing the actual work, they shared the gift of song with others who would in turn play the divine score on perfect cue. Hear it for yourself in God's soliloquy to Job.

Besides being sung on perfect cue, the songs of heaven are unceasingly sung—and never more vividly than when a person like you or like me is being delivered. Please sit up a little, shake the numbness from your head, and pay some extra mind as you read something else that the psalmist testified to his God: "You are my hiding place; you will protect me from trouble and surround me with songs of deliverance" (Psalm 32:7).

If music on earthly instruments and human tongues covers our arms with chill bumps, what does music sound like at the portals of heaven?!

Lord, the beauty of the crashing waves, the towering mountains, and the starry sky can call forth songs of praise. It's amazing that a person's deliverance, my deliverance, calls forth heavenly praise.

*I*f it's true that God surrounds us with songs of deliverance—and in Psalm 32:7 God Himself says it is—some of those very songs are playing right now. In fact, according to that Scripture, this whole book and every other one like it must be set to music we can't hear. If you've been in a pit, God wants nothing more for you than deliverance, and He has surrounded you with accompaniment on your journey out. Take it seriously. Think of the most dramatic movie you've ever seen and the thrilling score as the victory was won, the haunting notes as the lovers said farewell, or the building drama as the suspense built.

Now imagine something even better. Surely you don't think earthly movie producers and composers have anything on God. Every Oscar-winning expression of music is a mere echo of the God in whose image the clay-footed composer was created. Can you possibly think that God would deliver you in your real-life drama—a drama that engages both heaven and earth—without powerful accompaniment? Without poundings of percussion in the fury? Without weeping violins in the melancholy? Without trumpets of God in the victory? Without instruments you've never seen and sounds you've never heard? Not on your life. The originator of surround sound, God chases you down with melody and hems you in with harmony until your raptured soul finds liberty and your aching feet find stability. Christ, the King, the Creator of the Universe, seeks and surrounds *you* with songs of deliverance. Percussion, violins, trumpets, instruments I've never seen or heard—the music of heaven will be soul-satisfying beyond anything we can imagine!

Lord, may my heart be filled with Your song, reflecting Your joyful heavenly music in all that I do and say.

He put a new song in my mouth,
a hymn of praise to our God.
Many will see and fear the LORD
and put their trust in him.

Psalm 40:3

*G*od chases you down with melody and hems you in with harmony until your raptured soul finds liberty and your aching feet find stability. Christ, the King . . . seeks and surrounds you with songs of deliverance.

Can you let that truth sink into your swollen soul? Can you allow yourself to feel that loved? That sought? That significant? Maybe you and I will get to hear the scores accompanying each of our seasons of deliverance when we get to heaven. Picture Jesus handing us a personalized CD with a victorious scene from the final battle depicted on the front.

But now that I think about it, I hope it won't be just a CD. It needs to be a DVD. We won't just hear the music; we'll see the movie. We'll get to see the whole picture: the raging war in the unseen realm that took place over our heads as the angels of light fought the angels of darkness. We'll see exactly where Jesus was and what He was doing while every event unfolded. We'll hear the voice of God commanding the elements to cooperate. Our bonds to disintegrate. And, after all our waiting, we'll get to know the exact moment when God yelled, "Now!" If He holds the score that contains the songs of our deliverance, why wouldn't He also have the nonfiction movie that the songs were written for? After all, what's a score without a scene?

Until we get to heaven, we can sing by faith. After all, the music is playing. And who knows? Maybe our souls can hear what our ears can't discern.

Father, I'm so thankful that You are the author and composer of my life!

*L*ife leaves us in the dark about so many things. When we're little, we think we know what we want to be when we grow up, but when we're grown, many of us no longer have a clue. We walk down an aisle and promise "till death do us part," but God only knows who will part first. Our babies take their first steps to get to us, but we have no idea where life will really take them—or if they'll still like us when they get there. We're diagnosed with chronic diseases and coldly told the survival rates, but we have no clue where our number will fall in those statistics. We watch the news and squirm with the fresh realization that a sound mind isn't necessarily a requirement for becoming a world leader. We wonder how in heaven's name some maniac hasn't lost his mind and blown up the planet yet. If we live long enough and stay plugged in enough, we end up asking the same question our grandparents and parents asked: *What's this world coming to?* And we shake our heads as if no one has any idea.

God left a lot of questions unanswered—primarily, I imagine, because "without faith it is impossible to please God" (Hebrews 11:6). However, what this world is coming to is not unanswered. According to Revelation 21, earth as we know it will come to an end, and God will usher into existence a new heaven and a new earth with properties beyond our wildest imagination. God will dwell with man in a glorious new Jerusalem, and there "he will wipe every tear.... There will be no more death or mourning or crying or pain" (Revelation 21:4).

Lord God, I'm thankful to know that, even though I don't know all the answers to life's questions, I am loved and cherished by the One who is the answer to all of them.

*M*ost folks agree that heaven is a better option than
hell, but, comparatively speaking, only a handful
of Christians really anticipate their futures there. Face it.
We're scared to death that it's going to be like our church
services, only instead of getting out at noon, it will last an
eternity. For the life of us, we can't picture how anything
holy can possibly be lively. Let alone fun . . .

A few years ago I was studying Revelation 7 for a
series I was teaching, and God brought back to my mind
a familiar Old Testament passage using the same metaphor found in the passage I had just read. A wonderful
contrast jumped off the page at me and sent my imagination whirling. See it for yourself. The first passage refers
to life on earth. The second refers to life in heaven.

Psalm 23:1–3 says, "The LORD is my shepherd; I lack nothing. He makes me lie down in green pastures, he leads me beside quiet waters." Revelation 7:17 says, "For the Lamb at the center of the throne will be their shepherd; 'he will lead them to springs of living water.'"

Get a load of that: still waters on earth, but springs of living water in heaven. Compared to the white-water existence we'll have in heaven, here we're like toads perched on a lily pad in a stagnant pond. Despite our expectations, heaven is where all the action is. Our present existence, replete with every sunrise, sunset, season change, mountain range, forest glen, and foaming sea, is a mere shadow of an unthinkable reality.

Heaven is a reality I can't even begin to imagine, Lord God. It will reflect Your beauty, goodness, wisdom, and love in ways that will make this marvelous world pale in comparison. I'm so thankful to know I have a home there!

Whoever digs a hole and scoops it out
falls into the pit they have made.
The trouble they cause recoils on them;
their violence comes down on their own heads.

Psalm 7:15–16

I dearly love a great ending to a story, and you need to know that we will get one. The Author of our faith knows how to finish it.

As we wrap up this discussion of getting out of the pit, I want you to know what happens to the devil when all is said and done. It's such poetic justice. Revelation 20:1–3 describes it:

I saw an angel coming down out of heaven, having the key to the Abyss and holding in his hand a great chain. He seized the dragon, that ancient serpent, who is the devil, or Satan, and bound him for a thousand years. He threw him into the Abyss, and locked and sealed it over him, to keep him from deceiving the nations anymore until the thousand years were ended. After that, he must be set free for a short time.

There you have it. Before the Lord does away with Satan once and for all, He's going to give him a taste of the pit. It's the perfect plan, really. And sublimely scriptural. After all, look at what Psalm 7:15–16 promised long ago.

In God's economy, those who dig a pit for others will invariably fall into it themselves (Psalm 57:6). Hear Jesus speak about the end of the salvation story: "Behold, I am coming soon! My reward is with me, and I will give to everyone according to what he has done" (Revelation 22:12–13).

"And they lived happily ever after" is the fairy tale ending that doesn't happen on earth, but thank You, Lord, that Your children will indeed live happily ever after with You.

Our light and momentary troubles
are achieving for us an eternal glory
that far outweighs them all.

2 Corinthians 4:17

*G*od writes perfect endings. He can't help it. He's a wordsmith if you'll ever meet one. Every beginning will have a fitting ending. After all the dirt the prowling lion has gathered in his paws digging pits for us, he will eventually find himself caged in a pit. By the time Satan looks at life from a bottomless pit, our feet will forever be firmly set upon a rock. The air will be clear. The view, crystal. The fellowship, sweet. And the sufferings of this present time won't even be worthy of comparing to the glory revealed to us (Romans 8:18). We'll ride raftless in rivers of living water and bask in the Son.

Until then, life on this battered earth will not be easy, but we never have to make another bed in the bottom of a pit. We'll still have bad days. I had one yesterday and drank my sorrows to the dregs of my Starbuck's cappuccino. As I shook the cup to see if anything was left, my eyes fell on the quote: "It's tragic that extremists co-opt the notion of God, and that hipsters and artists reject spirituality out of hand. I don't have a fixed idea of God. But I feel that it's us—the messed-up, the half-crazy, the burning, the questing—that need God, a lot more than the goody-two-shoes do."[4]

I don't know anything about this guy or his theology. I just know I've been completely messed up and more than half crazy. And right there in the worst of it, while I was waist deep in the pit for what seemed the thousandth time, Christ stretched out His mighty arm, reached into the depths, and said in a way I could finally hear, "Need a hand?"

Grab Christ's hand. You'll never regret it.

Amazing grace. Unbounded love. Everlasting faithfulness. Great are You, Lord—and blessed am I!

---

4. Mike Doughty, *The Way I See It #158* (Starbucks Coffee Cup Series, 2006).

Notes

Notes

Notes

Notes

_____

_____

_____

_____

_____

_____

_____

_____

_____

_____

_____

_____

_____

_____

_____

_____

_____

_____

_____

Notes

_____
_____
_____
_____
_____
_____
_____
_____
_____
_____
_____
_____
_____
_____
_____
_____
_____
_____
_____

Notes

Notes